NEW YORK
YESTERDAY & TODAY

NEW YORK
Yesterday & Today

Meg Schneider

Voyageur Press

First published in 2008 by Voyageur Press, an imprint of
MBI Publishing Company and the Quayside Publishing Group,
400 First Avenue N, Suite 300, Minneapolis, MN 55401 USA

The information in this book is true and complete to the best
of our knowledge. All recommendations are made without
any guarantee on the part of the author or Publisher, who also
disclaim any liability incurred in connection with the use of this
data or specific details.

Voyageur Press titles are also available at discounts in bulk
quantity for industrial or sales-promotional use. For details
write to Special Sales Manager at MBI Publishing Company,
400 First Avenue N, Suite 300, Minneapolis, MN 55401 USA.

To find out more about our books, join us online at
www.voyageurpress.com.

Library of Congress Cataloging-in-Publication Data

Schneider, Meg Elaine.
  New York yesterday & today / text by Meg Schneider.
    p. cm.
  ISBN 978-0-7603-3065-4 (hb)
1. New York (State)—History—Pictorial works. 2. New York
(State)—Pictorial works. I. Title: New York yesterday and today.
  F120.S33 2008
  974.7—dc22

                         2008015177

On the front cover: (top) Lower Manhattan skyline, yesterday
and today; **(bottom)** maple sugaring in the Adirondacks.

On the back cover: (top) Syracuse, yesterday and today;
(right) vacationing in the Adirondacks, yesterday and today.

On the title page: Brooklyn Bridge, yesterday and today.

Editor: Josh Leventhal
Designer: Chris Fayers

Printed in China

Contents

Photo Credits 6
Preface and Acknowledgments 7
New York City: Capital City 8
Gateway to America 11
A Tale of Five Boroughs 14
Neighborhoods of New York 16
Wall Street 18
Greenwich Village 20
Washington Square 22
Union Square 24
Fifth Avenue 26
The Arts and Sciences 30
Times Square 32
Grand Central Terminal 34
Mass Transit 36
Harlem 38
Central Park 40
Coney Island 44
A Taste of New York 46
Long Island 48
The Catskills 50
Washington Irving 53
Sleepy Hollow 54
Bear Mountain 56
West Point 58
The Hudson Valley 60
Presidential Palaces 64
Kingston 66
Railroads 67
Albany 68
Troy 72
Saratoga Springs 74
Lake Champlain 76
Defending Land and Sea 78
The Adirondacks 80
Logging and Lumber 83
Great Camps of the Adirondacks 84
Saranac Lake 86
Lake Placid 88
Winter Sports 90
St. Lawrence Seaway 92
Castles of the Empire State 94
Erie Canal 96
The Mohawk Valley 98
Manufacturing and Small Industry 100
Utica – your dad worked in utica 101
Rome and Fort Stanwix 102
Cooperstown we lived 10 minutes from cooperstown 104
Baseball in New York 106
Football in New York 108
Basketball in New York 109
Syracuse 110
Great New York State Fair 112
Farming and Agriculture 114
Orchards and Vineyards 116
Finger Lakes 118
Seneca Falls 120
Watkins Glen 121
Ithaca 122
Corning 124
Religion in New York 126
Rochester 128
Chautauqua Lake 130
Native Americans in New York 132
Hunting and Fishing 134
Buffalo 136
Niagara Falls 138

Index 142
About the Author 144

Photo Credits

We wish to acknowledge the following for providing the photographs and illustrations included in the book. Every effort has been made to locate the copyright holders for materials used, and we apologize for any oversights. Archival material is from the Voyageur Press collection, unless otherwise noted.

Luke Bennett/Ambient Images: pp. 3, 9 top, 32, 38 top.

Peter Bennett/Ambient Images: pp. 2, 9 bottom, 13 bottom, 14 top right, 15 bottom, 17 bottom right, 21 bottom right, 27 top left, 30 bottom left, 33 top, 35 bottom, 39 both, 43 top, 45 top, 49 top right.

Jeffrey Greenberg/Ambient Images: pp. 85 top, 138 top.

Richard B. Levine/Ambient Images: p. 45 bottom.

Tony Perrottet/Ambient Images: p. 48 right.

Frances M. Roberts/Ambient Images: pp. 21 top right, 28 bottom, 36 bottom, 37.

Joseph A. Rosen/Ambient Images: pp. 27 right, 29 bottom, 31 bottom, 42 bottom, 46 top right.

Philip Scalia/Ambient Images: pp. 47, 52 bottom, 53 top, 59 bottom, 65 bottom, 66 right, 67 top right, 70, 71 top, 72 bottom, 73 top, 74 top right, 75 bottom, 79 bottom left, 87 bottom, 95 bottom, 97 both, 98 bottom, 99, 100 top right, 103 right, 104 bottom, 107 bottom right, 111 bottom, 117 bottom, 118 bottom, 119 top, 120 bottom right, 121 left, 123 top, 125 top left and bottom, 127 both, 129 top right, 131 top, 133 bottom.

Rick Shupper/Ambient Images: pp. 17 bottom left, 25 bottom, 41 bottom, 135 top.

J. Vasconcelos/Ambient Images: p. 10 bottom.

Jackie Weisberg/Ambient Images: pp. 49 bottom, 107 bottom left.

AP Images/Mark Lennihan: p. 107 top.

Diamond Images/Getty Images: p. 104 top.

Ben Liebenberg/NFL/Getty Images: p. 108 right.

Pro Football Hall of Fame/NFL/Getty Images: p. 108 left.

NBA Photos/Getty Images: p. 109 top right.

Ned Dishman/NBA/Getty Images: p. 109 bottom right.

The Granger Collection: pp. 20, 21 left, 22, 66 left, 96, 102 both, 116 both, 118 top, 120 top, 126, 132.

Carl Heilman II, Wild Visions, Inc.: pp. 35 top left, 51 both, 55 all, 56 bottom, 57, 58 bottom, 60 right, 61 top, 63 all, 69 top right and middle, 76 right, 77 bottom, 79 middle right, 81 both, 82 bottom, 83 bottom, 85 bottom, 86 top right, 89 middle and bottom, 90 bottom, 91 bottom left and right, 93 bottom, 94, 101 bottom, 103 left, 105, 113 both, 114 left, 117 top, 122 middle right, 125 top right, 129 bottom, 131 bottom, 134 right, 137 top right and bottom, 140 left, 141 top, front cover bottom.

Library of Congress, Prints & Photographs Division: pp. 8 top and lower right, 10 top, 11 top right, 12 both, 14 top left and bottom right, 15 top, 16 both, 17 top, 18 both, 19 left, 24 both, 25 top, 26, 27 bottom left, 28 top, 29 top, 31 top, 33 bottom, 34 both, 35 top right, 36 top left and right, 38 bottom, 40, 41 top left and top right, 43 bottom, 44 both, 46 top left, 48 left, 50 both, 52 top, 53 bottom, 54, 58 top, 59 top, 60 left, 61 bottom, 62, 64 both, 65 top, 67 top left and bottom right, 68 both, 69 top left and bottom, 72 top, 73 bottom, 74 top left and bottom, 75 top, 76 left, 77 top, 78, 79 top, 80 both, 82 top left, 83 top left and top right, 84 both, 86 bottom left, 87 top, 88 both, 90 top, 91 top left, 92 both, 95 top, 98 top, 100 top left and bottom right, 101 top, 106, 109 top left, 110, 111 top, 115 top, 122 top, 123 bottom, 124, 128 both, 129 top left, 130 both, 133 top, 135 bottom, 136 both, 137 top left, 138 bottom, 139, 141 bottom, front cover top left.

George Ostertag: pp. 13 top, 114 right, 115 bottom, 120 bottom left.

Shutterstock: pp. 11 bottom left and bottom right, 19 right, 23, 46 bottom, front cover top right.

Preface and Acknowledgments

When I was twelve or thirteen years old, I announced to my family that history was boring. My father, the history teacher, didn't take it well; I believe he felt he had failed as a parent. A few years later, Dad took me to Appomattox in Virginia, where a National Park Service employee in the role of a Rebel soldier helped me understand for the first time my father's fascination with the past. Since then, it has been a fascination I share.

New York is an exceptionally rich place to indulge such interests. Sometimes when I'm driving, I try to imagine what the landscape must have looked like to the Indians of five hundred or a thousand years ago, when virtually the entire state was thickly forested and populated more with beaver, deer, and wild turkey than with people. I think of the Iroquois tradition of offering thanks to the Creator and all the gifts he has provided, and how this wilderness must have seemed like paradise, abundant in all that they needed.

To the European explorers, it was a different kind of paradise, a land of seemingly inexhaustible resources on which could be built fortunes beyond the dreams of avarice. To the colonists, it was a land of unheard-of freedom, and it took only a few generations for that newfound independence to become the keystone of our national heritage. New York was ravaged by the American Revolution, but this is where that war was won—in a muddy ravine at Oriskany, at Fort Ticonderoga, in Westchester, and on Long Island. New Yorkers and their Oneida allies stymied the mighty British here, and for the first time in the world's history, a collection of colonies broke free from the parent sovereign and set about establishing its own empire.

Native New Yorkers boast that there is no need to leave the state because anything you could want is right here: the most fascinating city in the world, the rugged grace of the Adirondacks, the bucolic splendor of the Finger Lakes, the raw beauty of the Great Lakes and Niagara Falls, and always right in front of you, the history that brought us to this point. If you can't find something in the Empire State to pique your interest, you must be jaded indeed.

With the easy arrogance common to authors, I will doubtless refer to this as "my" book whenever the occasion arises. In truth, many people have just as valid a claim to ownership—some, perhaps, even more than me. First on this list is editor Josh Leventhal, with whom the idea originated and who permanently endeared himself to me when he apologized for giving me only (!) six months to complete the manuscript. Next is my agent, Barb Doyen, who combines a touching faith in my abilities with an uncanny knack for finding interesting projects for me. Mark Dixon earns kudos for keeping me on track and taking care of everything else while I'm buried in research and writing; I can't say whether I'm more grateful for the support or for his willingness to put up with all the loopiness that so often accents a writer's life. Finally, Dick and Jan Schneider—Dad, thanks for encouraging my curiosity, and Mom, thanks for sharing adventures and explorations with me.

Meg Schneider
Cleveland, New York

Lower Manhattan skyline, 1911

New York City: Capital City

Since long before it was known as Gotham, The Big Apple, or even New Amsterdam, New York City has always been the capital of something. The Lenape Indians, whose ancestors hunted, trapped, and fished on the islands in and around New York Harbor, had been cultivating crops on Manhattan and conducting a trading center in what is now the West Village for centuries by the time the first European explorers arrived in the 1500s. (European colonists later gave the Lenape the more familiar name of the Delaware.) The Dutch West India Company carried on the trading tradition, making New Amsterdam the commerce capital of the New World, as did the English when they took over and renamed the settlement New York. In 1792, a group of merchants and stockbrokers signed an agreement beneath the shade of a buttonwood (or sycamore) tree, creating the forerunner of the New York Stock Exchange.

American theater was born here in 1750 with the staging of *Richard III*, and other performing arts—dance, opera, symphony, and even movies—can trace their American roots to the small island the Lenape called Manhattan. The fashion industry established itself in the three decades leading up to the Civil War, when the manufacture of clothing was the city's fastest growing industry.

When the federal government took control of immigration functions in the late 1800s, New York Harbor became America's front door, the entry point for millions of people in search of a better life in the land of opportunity.

And although it served as the nation's capital for just one year (George Washington was inaugurated at Federal Hall in 1789, and James Madison proposed the Bill of Rights in the same building) and as the state capital for only fourteen years, New York City has always wielded enormous political clout at home and abroad.

Map of New York City, 1878

Lower Manhattan skyline, 1947

Lower Manhattan skyline, 2007

Throughout its history, New York City also has been the capital of contrasts and contradictions. The Native Americans were eager to trade with the Europeans but less than thrilled with the unintended consequences of that relationship. The Dutch promoted international trade at the same time it built forts for protection against foreign invaders. In colonial times, pigs and landed gentry traveled the same muddy roads. Vaudeville sprouted up next to the legitimate theater. Crime and commerce, wealth and poverty, vice and virtue: New York City has always had it all and has been variously lauded and ridiculed for its multiple facets and inherent dichotomy. The Swiss architect Le Corbusier allowed that New York was a "catastrophe," but "a beautiful catastrophe." Mayor John Lindsay likened his city to an entire array of cooking appliances: "Not only is New York the nation's melting pot, it is also the casserole, the chafing dish, and the charcoal grill."

The city's official seal reflects its diverse history. The seal depicts a sailor and an Indian flanking a shield that shows the arms of a windmill, two flour barrels, and two beavers; an eagle with spread wings sits atop a hemisphere. The seal also bears the number 1625, the year New Amsterdam was founded.

Right: *Midtown Manhattan skyline, 1931*

Below: *Midtown Manhattan skyline*

GATEWAY TO AMERICA

If you stand quietly in the vast main building of the Ellis Island Immigration Museum and let the low rumble of your fellow visitors' conversation eddy around you, you can almost transport yourself back one hundred years or so and imagine that the voices belong to some of the 12 million people who began their American experience on this three-acre erstwhile oyster bed.

Together, the Statue of Liberty in New York Harbor and Ellis Island are inextricably linked as icons of the great wave of immigrants that poured into America in the 1890s and early 1900s. But both achieved their status more through circumstance than design.

The Statue of Liberty was conceived as a political statement; it was supposed to represent France's vision of its own place in history as a democracy. But Emma Lazarus' poem on the statue's base and the mass emigration of Europe's poorest, most desperate denizens soon transformed Liberty Enlightening the World (as the statue was formally named) into a symbol of a new life in a new country. Historians note that most of the immigrants of the 1890s and early 1900s saw themselves as Lazarus' poem described them: tired, poor, homeless, tempest tossed.

Statue of Liberty, 1894

Ellis Island and Liberty Island

Statue of Liberty

Between 1892 and 1954, an average of 5,000 immigrants a day walked into the main building at Ellis Island; on a single day in 1907, nearly 12,000 arrived here. Virtually all of them were poor. First- and second-class steamship passengers were presumed to present little risk of becoming a burden on the government and were allowed to bypass the inspection process at Ellis Island; only those unfortunate souls in steerage were deemed suspect. Those who passed the medical and legal inspections (and the vast majority of them did pass, as a scant 250,000 out of 12 million were turned away) were allowed to continue their journey inside America's borders. About one-third of them remained in the New York City area, and the rest fanned out across the nation to join relatives or friends and begin building their lives anew.

Ellis Island National Monument

A half century has passed since Ellis Island processed its last immigrant, but more than 100 million Americans can trace their family's roots in the New World to this spot. After being neglected and allowed to fall into a disgraceful state of decay over some forty years, the restored Main Building opened as an immigration museum on September 10, 1990. Today, the American Family Immigration History Center allows professional and amateur genealogists to search passenger records from 1892 to 1924. The American Immigrant Wall of Honor, built outside the main building and paid for with private donations, lists the names of about 600,000 immigrants.

Opposite, top: *Immigrant Landing Station, Ellis Island, 1905*

Opposite, bottom: *Immigrants arriving at Ellis Island*

Tourists arriving at Ellis Island Immigration Museum

"Staten Island and the Narrows," Currier and Ives lithograph, 1861

Historic Richmond Town, Staten Island

A TALE OF FIVE BOROUGHS

For most people, the words "New York City" conjure up a mental picture of the skyscrapers and busy streets of Manhattan. But, just as the Upper West Side differs in personality and ambience from Midtown and Midtown looks and feels nothing like the Battery, the five boroughs that make up the whole of the city have distinct—and continually evolving—personalities.

Surviving Dutch, English, and French records from the seventeenth century spell "Manhattan" dozens of ways, and there are several stories as to the origin of the name. One story contends that it is a Dutch interpretation of the name the Indians living on the island gave themselves: the "Manna-hatta." Another story says it's a Lenape word that means, depending on which translation you accept, "high island," "island of hills," or simply "island." The "high island" version comes from a tale—possibly true, but also possibly not—that Henry Hudson gave brandy to an Indian leader, who passed out; after waking, the leader asked Hudson to share the brandy with other members of his tribe.

The origins of the other borough names are clearer. The Bronx takes its name from a Danish landholder names Jonas Bronck, who purchased five hundred acres of land north of Manhattan in 1639; the estate was referred to as The Broncks'. Staten Island also was an estate; when the estate failed and its owner went bankrupt, ownership of the island was transferred to the Dutch government,

or *Staaten General*. Queens was named for Catherine of Braganza, wife of King Charles II of England. And the Dutch named Brooklyn after a village in the Netherlands, Breukelen. The name is translated as either "broken land" or "marshland."

Although all the boroughs—even Manhattan—entered the European consciousness as farming and hunting land, it's difficult to envision any neighborhood in today's sprawling city as anything other than part of a great metropolis. Most vestiges of New York City's agrarian beginnings have faded so as to be more or less meaningless now; few people know, for instance, that the Bowery neighborhood in Manhattan got its name from the Dutch word for "farms."

Brooklyn Bridge and Lower Manhattan

Seaside Avenue, Rockaway, Queens, 1904

Below: *Grand Concourse, The Bronx*

NEIGHBORHOODS OF NEW YORK

New York City has always attracted people from a broad spectrum of backgrounds. Records from the mid-1600s show that the area's 1,500 residents were not just Dutch and English, but Flemish, German, Danish, French Huguenot, Swedish, and African as well. Thirty years before the biggest human migration in modern history began to flood Ellis Island, half the city's residents were foreign born.

Still, the concept of America as a great "melting pot," where people from numerous cultures and backgrounds intermingled to form a new national identity, has always been more mythic ideal than reality. When the English took over New Amsterdam and renamed it New York, the Dutch settlers tended to live among themselves in close-knit communities. Later immigrants followed suit, settling in neighborhoods that were defined less by physical boundaries than by ties of language and national, ethnic, or religious heritage. There was both safety and comfort in numbers. In a land where nothing was familiar, living among one's countrymen held at least the promise of mutual understanding, assistance, and loyalty.

Thus grew New York's now-famous Little Italy, Chinatown, and other neighborhoods, all of which have evolved over the decades as some groups moved out and others moved in.

Lower East Side, 1907

Manhattan's Lower East Side became home to thousands of immigrants, jammed into tenements and crowding the streets with homemade vendor bags and push carts. Financially, most of them were poor, but culturally they brought untold wealth with them from their homelands—riches that have made these neighborhoods bona fide tourist attractions today. Food and festivals abound, and savvy shoppers prowl the cramped boutiques looking for their own treasures among a cornucopia of authentic handmade and imported goods and cheap knockoffs.

Those looking for less touristy ethnic neighborhoods may be more interested in places like Brighton Beach, where you're more likely to hear conversations in Russian than in English, or Ditmas Park in Brooklyn, one of the few neighborhoods that actually reflects the "melting pot" ideal of people from diverse backgrounds living together as a cohesive community.

Street vendor, Italian feast, Little Italy, circa 1910

Port Arthur Restaurant, Chinatown, circa 1913

Little India, Jackson Heights, Queens

Dragon dance, Chinatown

WALL STREET

Wall Street, toward Trinity Church, 1847

Today, most allusions to "Wall Street" refer to global finance and the stock market more than to the actual street in New York City. Ever since two dozen merchants and stockbrokers signed the Buttonwood Agreement—the forerunner of the New York Stock Exchange—beneath a sycamore, or buttonwood, tree on the southern end of Manhattan in 1792, Wall Street has been the center of American financial activity.

It has been, by no measure, a serene two hundred years for the fabled Financial District. The Great Fire of 1776 destroyed many buildings on the southern end of Manhattan, including the original Trinity Church, built on Wall Street in 1698. Another Great Fire, this one in 1835, destroyed nearly seven hundred buildings, and only three of the city's twenty-six fire insurance companies survived the disaster without going bankrupt. The September 11, 2001, terrorist attacks brought down the World Trade Center, and the rebuilding process has been slowed by both political and financial struggles.

Physical disasters like these have been rarer than financial ones over the years. The vagaries of the local, national, and world economies have wrought havoc on countless personal and corporate fortunes. Wall Street endured the Panic of 1837—during which time novelist Washington Irving spoke disparagingly of the "almighty dollar"—only to have it return even more ferociously two decades later; twenty banks and ten thousand businesses

Wall Street, 1884 Panic

failed during the Panic of 1857, and troops were called in to quell riots by workers who were protesting not just the lack of jobs but a serious food shortage.

Robber barons trying to corner the gold market caused the stock market to crash in 1869, and the New York Stock Exchange closed for ten days in 1873 when financial markets went haywire. In 1893, the stock market nosedived on June 27, and the nation entered a four-year depression. Thirty-six years later, another crash ushered in the Great Depression of the 1930s.

New York Stock Exchange, 1908

New York Stock Exchange and statue of George Washington

In the 1940s, Charles E. Merrill began introducing the middle class to investing; his company, Merrill Lynch, opened one hundred branches around the country as part of a campaign "to bring Wall Street to Main Street." Since then, and with the introduction of stock-based 401(k) plans and Individual Retirement Accounts (IRAs), Wall Street's performance has been watched carefully not just by corporate boards of directors, but by millions of Americans whose financial security depends largely on how healthy the stock market is.

The market turned out to be not so healthy on October 19, 1987, a day that has come to be known as Black Monday. The Dow Jones Industrial Average fell by more than 22 percent in a single day, the biggest one-day decline in history. The crash had worldwide ramifications, and it took the stock market years to bounce back. Smaller crashes have occurred since then, but investors from around the world continue to look to Wall Street as a bellwether of the global economy.

Lodging for the poor, Greenwich Village, 1869

GREENWICH VILLAGE

Historically, the pendulum in Greenwich Village has swung between fashionable and anti-establishment. Originally a marshland where Native Americans fished in Minetta Brook, the Dutch and freed African slaves turned it into farmland, and the English, taking advantage of its distance from the population center on Lower Manhattan, turned what is now Washington Square into a cemetery for indigents and a public hanging square. The neighborhood was only sparsely populated until the 1800s, when cholera and yellow fever outbreaks forced many to flee the crowded conditions of Lower Manhattan for the pastoral peace of Greenwich Village.

It was those health concerns that prompted many Manhattanites to remain in Greenwich Village, and the swelling population there led developers to fill in marshy spots, divide farm plots, and build streets of row houses to shelter the area's new permanent residents. Educational, religious, and cultural institutions sprang up virtually overnight. New York University was soon joined by countless art clubs, libraries, picture galleries, and literary salons, juxtaposed with high-end shops, hotels, restaurants, and theaters.

At the turn of the twentieth century, Greenwich Village lost its affluent character as working-class German, Italian, and Irish immigrants moved in to take jobs in the lumber and coal yards, breweries, and warehouses along the Hudson River. Wealthy residents moved farther uptown, and their homes were converted into apartments and cheap residential hotels. By World War I, Greenwich Village was known as a bohemian center, ethnically diverse, embracing the avant-garde, the radical, and the

Street art sale, Macdougal Alley, 1950s

Upscale retail shops, Bleecker Street

Blue Note jazz club, West 3rd Street

nonconforming. Its idiosyncrasies made it popular with tourists, and the pendulum was swinging back toward the fashionable when the stock market crash of 1929 halted construction of new luxury buildings aimed at the well-to-do.

The Village was a center for beatniks in the 1950s, for gays and lesbians in the 1960s, for antiwar protestors in the 1970s, and for AIDS activists in the 1980s. By the 1990s, the Village was the place to be for wealthy intellectuals, and demand for housing sent rents so high that the iconic "brilliant starving artists" so long associated with Greenwich Village could no longer afford to live there. Still, it remains a wonderful neighborhood, with its coffee shops and secluded streets and nightly "happenings" featuring musicians, poets, and artists of all types.

Washington Square arch, 1891

WASHINGTON SQUARE

With its iconic marble arch and central fountain, Washington Square is one of the best-known parks in New York City. It has been featured in countless films: Meg Ryan dropped Billy Crystal off in front of the arch in *When Harry Met Sally*; Jeff Goldblum played chess with Judd Hirsch at one of the outdoor chess tables in *Independence Day*; and Will Smith's character in 2008's *I Am Legend* lived and worked in the Washington Square neighborhood. A slightly different perspective of this historic neighborhood was provided by Henry James, whose classic 1880 novel *Washington Square* depicted the societal mores and familial relationships surrounding a late-nineteenth-century New York family.

Originally part of the farmland cultivated by Native American and Dutch settlers, the ten or so acres that make up Washington Square today were purchased by the city in the late eighteenth century for use as a potter's field for the city's poor or unknown. Because it was then outside the city limits, it later became the

Street performer, Washington Square

burial ground for victims of yellow fever, as part of a postmortem quarantine policy. The cemetery was closed in 1825, and in 1827, it was converted to a public park and military parade ground, where troops practiced drills.

The marble arch, which was modeled after the Arc de Triomphe in Paris, was installed in 1895 to replace a wooden one that had been erected in 1889 to mark the one-hundredth anniversary of George Washington's inauguration as president.

In the twentieth century, Washington Square became a hub for rallies, memorials, and protests. Some 20,000 workers marched to the park in 1912 to commemorate the first anniversary of the infamous Triangle Shirtwaist Factory fire, in which nearly 150 people died. Three years later, more than 25,000 people marched to demand voting rights for women. In 2008, Democratic presidential candidate Barack Obama held a rally here, and the crowd, numbering more than 20,000, overran the cordon that police had set up for the event.

For the last fifty years or so, Washington Square has been a magnet for the bohemian and arty crowd that has made its home in Greenwich Village, and tensions between the city's establishment and area residents are never far below the surface. Park preservation groups have held candlelight vigils and rallies to protest the city's redesign of the park, which includes plans to cut down trees, make the central plaza smaller, and change the fountain design.

UNION SQUARE

Union Square, 1910

In 1861, Union Square was the site of what was believed to be the largest political gathering ever in North America: a massive rally pledging the city's support to the North at the beginning of the Civil War. But the square derives its name not from this rally, nor from the many labor parades and demonstrations that it has seen over the years. Rather, it is named for geography; it's located at the point where Broadway (then known as Bloomingdale Road) met another then-important (and now nonexistent) thoroughfare called East Post Road.

Union Square has always been a draw for protestors, demonstrations, and radical speakers. Emma Goldman, a Russian-American anarchist, told 3,000 people at a rally here that they should steal bread if they could not afford to buy it. The first Labor Day celebration, in 1882, brought a parade of some 10,000 workers past the reviewing stand at the park. On May Day in 1908, thousands convened at Union Square for a Socialist Party gathering. Nearly a century later, following the terrorist attacks in New York, Washington, and Pennsylvania on September 11, 2001, Union Square became a spontaneous memorial zone, where stunned and mourning New Yorkers set up impromptu vigils and displays of candles, flowers, pictures, and other memorabilia.

In happier times, Union Square is home to an expansive Greenmarket. Every Monday, Wednesday, Friday, and Saturday throughout the year, regional farmers sell their varied produce to an average of 250,000 customers a week. Between Thanksgiving and Christmas, the Greenmarket is augmented by the annual Holiday Market, where more than 1,000 artisans sell gifts from temporary booths, stalls, and kiosks.

Socialist rally at Union Square, 1908

Greenmarket, Union Square

FIFTH AVENUE

New York Public Library, Fifth Avenue and 42nd Street, circa 1908

Millionaires' Row, Museum Mile, the Most Expensive Shopping District in the World—New York City's Fifth Avenue has worn many posh monikers over the years. Edith Wharton immortalized the Victorian Era wealth and society of Fifth Avenue in her Pulitzer Prize–winning novel, *The Age of Innocence*.

Wealthy powerbrokers in New York City established the avenue's toniness as early as the 1860s, when Caroline Schermerhorn Astor built her home on the corner of Fifth Avenue and 34th Street. From there, the millionaires moved northward, particularly coveting spots facing Central Park, between 59th and 96th Streets. Still today, most of the residences on that stretch of Fifth Avenue date from the 1920s. Only a few buildings betray post–World War II facades, the most notable being the Solomon R. Guggenheim Museum, which was designed in the 1940s and '50s by Frank Lloyd Wright, but was not completed until 1959, after both he and Guggenheim had died.

South of Central Park, Fifth Avenue lost its residential flavor around the turn of the twentieth century, when Benjamin Altman built his department store on Fifth and 34th, kitty-corner from the Astor mansion. (The Astor mansion was knocked down in 1890 to make room for the original Waldorf-Astoria Hotel, which,

New York Public Library, Fifth Avenue and 42nd Street

Trump Tower, Fifth Avenue and 56th Street

Fifth Avenue and 51st Street, 1907

in its turn, was demolished to make room for the Empire State Building.) Altman's department store took up the frontage of the entire block and thereby founded the high-end shopping district Fifth Avenue is known for around the world today. Tiffany's, Saks, Cartier, and Lord & Taylor are here; also among its notable retail residents are the renowned F.A.O. Schwartz, Abercrombie & Fitch's flagship store, and the thirty-two-foot-tall glass cube that serves as the entrance to Apple's flagship retail outlet, which is completely underground.

Other New York City icons grace Fifth Avenue as well, including the New York Public Library with its twin stone lions; Rockefeller Center, with its ice skating rink and nationally televised Christmas tree-lighting ceremony; and St. Patrick's Cathedral, as well as more recent additions to the avenue's rich cache, such as Trump Tower.

Poster advertising Fifth Avenue, "the world's greatest shopping street," 1932

Christmas shoppers on Fifth Avenue

Left: *Children admiring display of Christmas toys in Macy's window, circa 1910s*

Below: *Christmas display, Saks Fifth Avenue*

For the past 250 years, New York City has been a haven for the arts. Shakespeare's *Richard III* was performed for the first time in the New World in 1750; Lorenzo da Ponte, librettist for several of Mozart's operas, including *Don Giovanni* and *The Marriage of Figaro*, inspired the building of New York's Italian Opera House in the early 1800s; and the New York Philharmonic gave its first concert in 1842.

The American Museum of Natural History, originally housed in Central Park's arsenal, has been thrilling schoolchildren and adults with its enormous collection of dinosaur bones and other fossils, not to mention its lifelike dioramas and science exhibits, from its quarters on Central Park West since 1877. The collections cover virtually every discipline in human scientific research and discovery, from biology and anthropology to geology

Postcard view of the Museum of Natural History

and astronomy. There's even something for those interested in different architectural styles. The entrance on Central Park West has imposing stone columns and a bronze statue of Theodore Roosevelt on a horse; other parts of the building resemble a fairy-tale castle, and the Rose Center for Earth and Space is a modern structure of glass and metal.

While many of New York City's museums are dedicated to specific types of art—folk art, photography, textiles, and of course, modern art—the Metropolitan Museum of Art has always prided itself on its universal collection. The Met has works in every possible medium from virtually every point in geography and recorded time, and its displays are arranged to facilitate comparison among peoples, cultures, and eras. Among its best-known exhibits is an entire Egyptian temple, which was shipped to the United States as a gift.

The Lincoln Center for the Performing Arts is the hub for dance, music, film, and theater. It is home to eleven resident performing arts organizations, ranging from the Metropolitan Opera and the New York City Ballet to the Film Society, the Chamber Music Society, and the world-famous Juilliard School. In all, Lincoln Center presents more than 400 events a year for nearly five million visitors. The Lincoln Center Institute also offers educational and family arts-related programs throughout the city.

Rose Center, Hayden Planetarium, Museum of Natural History

Above: *Metropolitan Museum of Art, 1914*

Metropolitan Museum of Art

Times Square, 1948

TIMES SQUARE

Times Square may be the only place in the United States where advertisers can be fined if their signs aren't bright enough. As part of a twenty-year effort to clean up Times Square and make it a place where businesses, residents, and tourists want to be, the city's zoning laws contain a term not found anywhere else: the LUTS, or "Light Unit Times Square." There are regulations for minimum LUTS readings for the glitzy electronic signs that adorn virtually every square inch of every building in the neighborhood. The "spectaculars"—the apt name given to the oversized electric signs that made their first appearances before World War I—are huge revenue generators; rents for such signs run hundreds of thousands of dollars a month.

Like many other New York City neighborhoods, Times Square has had its good and bad decades. In the 1900s and teens, it was an amalgamation of Ziegfeld Follies, rooftop gardens, and shamelessly indulgent wining and dining; in the 1920s, it was flappers and speakeasies; in the 1930s, it was the moxie glamour of hardworking chorus girls interspersed with nickel movies and dime museums.

The end of World War II was the beginning of Times Square's descent into debauchery. Always skating along the fine line between harmless blowing-off-steam fun and really naughty, the neighborhood lost its balance as hookers, peep shows, and porn shops began taking up residence. Con artists and drug dealers followed, and by the 1970s, Times Square was as dirty and dangerous a place as you could imagine. Assault, armed robbery, and murder were, by no exaggeration, daily occurrences. During this period, Harlem recorded only a third as many total felonies as Times Square. It was the poster child for everything that was wrong with America's cities.

It took twenty years and three mayoral administrations to turn things around. Ed Koch started the process with a plan to move the indulgent-but-respectable aspects of Times Square *away*

Times Square, 1998

from Times Square itself. Of course, this plan didn't go anywhere, but it did get people talking about what could and should be done to clean up the neighborhood. By the 1990s, then-mayor Rudolph Giuliani cut the ribbon on the "new" Times Square, sharing the credit with corporate giants such as Disney and Toys R Us and leaving critics to decry this Times Square as a mere corporate impersonation of its former glory. They bemoan the loss of the square's quirkiness, the independent shops catering to narrow niches of clientele, the weirdness that gave these few blocks their unique personality.

On the other hand, today's Times Square is, as it always has been, the center of commercial culture. The world's busiest McDonald's is here, along with Applebee's and dozens of other national and international chains. It still pulses with the energy of theaters and showrooms, business types and tourists, cabs and limos and private cars. It still celebrates on-the-verge-of-naughty indulgence. And it's still a great backdrop for a vacation photo.

Long Acre (later Times) Square, 1911

GRAND CENTRAL TERMINAL

Grand Central Terminal owes its survival to the demolition of the original Pennsylvania Station in the 1960s. Public outcry over the destruction of one of the city's best-known landmarks led to the creation of the City Landmarks Preservation Commission, which placed Grand Central under legal protection as a historic site and helped prevent a number of proposed projects that would have jeopardized the facade, the interior, or even the very existence of railroad baron Cornelius Vanderbilt's "vast marble palace."

The palace opened in 1913 to replace an old depot that combined the operations of three separate railroads. Grand Central featured sixty-seven tracks on two levels and was designed to handle the movement of 70,000 people an hour. Construction took ten years, and the new terminal was so highly anticipated that 150,000 people turned out to see it the day it opened. More than a mere train station, Grand Central was a center for news, art, and education. It at one time housed a newsreel theater, an art gallery and an art school, a railroad museum, and countless exhibitions.

In 1998, after four years and $425 million, Grand Central was returned to its original splendor—and then some. It's still a train station, but Grand Central is a destination in itself for locals and tourists alike, featuring more than two dozen restaurants, lounges, and snack bars; fifty specialty shops; and the gourmet Grand Central Market. The former main waiting room, now dubbed Vanderbilt Hall, offers entertainment and exhibits and hosts an annual Holiday Fair of artisans and importers offering gifts for sale.

New Grand Central Terminal, 1914

Interior, Grand Central Terminal

Interior, Grand Central Terminal, circa 1940s

Grand Central Terminal at night

Horse-drawn streetcars, Broadway, 1892

Elevated train, 1895

MASS TRANSIT

Getting people around New York City safely has always been a challenge. As early as 1850, traffic jams were a regular occurrence on Broadway. In 1853, the city had to ban the practice of herding cattle to slaughterhouses south of 42nd Street during daylight hours.

The first public transportation in the city appeared in the late 1820s in the form of "accommodations"—horse-drawn buses that could carry up to twelve passengers. These shortly gave way to larger vehicles, still drawn by horses, with seating for thirty people. Still, by the post–Civil War era, the streets of New York were so crowded that the city began to build elevated tracks (els) for steam-powered trains to try to relieve the congestion, creating the first rapid-transit system in the country. During its peak year of 1921, the els carried 384 million passengers.

The subway system was seen as a threat to streetcars, whose operators paid kickbacks to Mayor Boss Tweed, but development went ahead, often in secret, funded by wealthy entrepreneurs. In 1894, city residents overwhelmingly voted for an ambitious subway system, and over the next thirty years, some 30,000 men

Hybrid-electric bus, Harlem

Subway platform at rush hour, Fulton Street Station

dug the trenches and tunnels for it. The work was often done by hand; steam shovels weren't sufficiently maneuverable to avoid the confusing mass of underground pipes and wires.

In 1908, the subway went under the East River to connect Manhattan and Brooklyn and over the Harlem River to connect Manhattan and The Bronx. Two years later, Pennsylvania Station opened in Midtown, and its more famous sister station, the "vast marble palace" of Grand Central Terminal, opened in 1913.

Meanwhile, the city took over the Staten Island Ferry and bought five new boats, named after the city's boroughs. Until 1972, a ride cost only a nickel. The fare for foot passengers was raised first to a dime, then to a quarter, and finally to fifty cents before the fare was abolished altogether in 1997.

Taxis with gas engines appeared on New York's streets in the early 1900s, and almost immediately drivers went on strike, demanding a union and better pay—a none-too-rare event even today for transit workers.

In the 1950s and '60s, Midtown streets were changed to one-way streets in an effort to speed up traffic. In 2007, Mayor Michael Bloomberg proposed a "congestion pricing" plan, similar to a program in use in London, to ease traffic snarls in Manhattan by charging private cars a fee to enter the central business district on weekdays. The proposal has the support of the federal government and several environmental groups, but others oppose it on various grounds.

In the 1980s and '90s, the city spent $1 billion fixing up subway trains and tracks, after a decade or more of little investment. The ubiquitous graffiti that many subway cars and stations sported in the 1970s is rare now, and, since 1990, most subway cars have air conditioning, making the commute in warm weather much more comfortable for the city's approximately five million daily straphangers. The city continues to invest in improving its public transportation system; in 2008, officials announced $14 million in improvements to subway and bus service in The Bronx.

125th Street and Eighth Avenue, Harlem, 1948

HARLEM

At various points in its history, Harlem has represented both the vibrant creative center of jazz and other musical forms, and the epitome of urban blight, poverty, and economic racism. In truth, this neighborhood has been both these things and more through its complex history. The Dutch named the area *Nieuw Haarlem* after a place in Holland, but English immigrants shortened the name to Harlem. It was an agricultural enclave until the elevated trains extended to the area around the turn of the twentieth century. By 1910, Harlem's population had swelled to a half million people.

It was by no means an African American neighborhood then. Only about 10 percent of the residents in 1910 were black; the rest were primarily immigrants from Europe and Russia. In the early days of the twentieth century, Yiddish signs were common in Harlem, speaking to the large Jewish population.

African Americans began to move to Harlem in large numbers in the 1920s and '30s, taking advantage of the miscalculations of speculative builders. With houses and apartments standing empty, these developers were forced to open their previously restricted rentals to people of all races, and blacks quickly filled the vacancies. By the 1930s, 200,000 African Americans were living in Harlem.

During the era from Prohibition through World War II, Harlem was the center for jazz and blues. The Cotton Club and the

Civil rights march, Harlem, 1965

Apollo Theater launched the careers of some of the biggest names in music: Duke Ellington, Louis Armstrong, Ella Fitzgerald, Billie Holiday, and Cab Calloway. While few blacks could see these stars in person—only whites were typically allowed into these clubs to watch the performances—radio broadcasts brought their

125th Street and Frederick Douglass Boulevard (Eighth Avenue), Harlem

music into the living rooms of millions. The original Cotton Club closed in 1940, although it was resurrected in another location in 1978. The Apollo is still a major venue for established and emerging performers.

In the 1960s and '70s, civil rights protests and race riots often dominated the national news about Harlem. The area earned an unsavory reputation as a crowded, unsanitary, and unsafe community. The Committee on Racial Equality (CORE) was established to act as a liaison between city officials and Harlem residents; it was particularly active on the issue of police abuse toward blacks and other minorities.

Since the 1990s, Harlem has been enjoying an economic and cultural renaissance, with new businesses on the increase and crime on the decline. Columbia University has purchased large swaths of Harlem, bringing renewed interest in the area from developers and middle-class newcomers, who have renovated and restored some of Harlem's most significant architecture. The gentrification of this once-decaying neighborhood has not been without controversy, though. Now that people are willing to pay market rates for housing in Harlem, many of the working poor have been forced out. The city's eternal battle between affluence and affordability has begun a new cycle in this area.

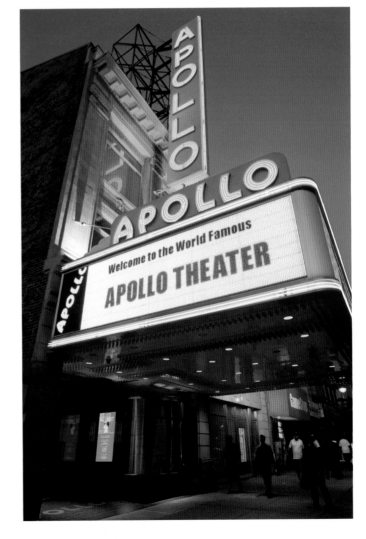

Apollo Theater, 125th Street

Birdseye view of Central Park, 1859

CENTRAL PARK

The first landscaped public park in the United States, Central Park was conceived as a necessary amenity to place New York among the great cities of the world. Proponents argued that it would provide open space for the poor, but in fact its creation involved displacing about 1,600 poor residents, mainly Irish and German immigrants who lived in shanties on the swampy terrain, as well as an African American community called Seneca Village. By the time construction on the park was under way in the late 1850s, few of Manhattan's poor could afford the fare uptown to enjoy it.

The city conducted an open contest to design the park, and the winners were American landscape designer Frederick Law Olmstead and the English-born architect Calvert Vaux. Olmstead and Vaux collaborated on a "greensward" plan to convert the property into a magnificent park. Implementing their plan involved 20,000 workers, who moved about 3 million cubic yards of earth and planted more than a quarter million shrubs and trees. The park took twenty years to complete.

In 1880, Egypt donated Cleopatra's Needle to the United States, and the seventy-foot obelisk, which dates from 1475 BC, was rolled on cannonballs from the Hudson River to Central Park. Around the same time, Sunday afternoon concerts were introduced in the park, and other attractions, including the carousel and zoo, quickly became popular features.

The park's design and amenities continue to be shaped by the people who use it. Playgrounds and athletic fields, skating rinks, and paths for walking, jogging, inline skating, and bicycling all have been added over the years in response to New Yorkers' demands. In 1981, a few months after John Lennon was fatally shot outside the Dakota apartment building across the street from the park, a section of the park near West 72nd Street was renamed Strawberry Fields in honor of the former Beatle. Each year on December 8, the anniversary of his death, fans gather to pay their respects to Lennon's memory with flowers, candles, and performances of his music.

May Day celebration, Central Park, 1907

Lover's Lane, Central Park, 1896

Sheep Meadow, Central Park, 2008

*Postcard view of Bethesda Fountain,
Central Park, circa 1908*

Bethesda Fountain, Central Park

Boating on lake, Central Park

Boating on lake, Central Park, Currier and Ives lithograph, late nineteenth century

CONEY ISLAND

Coney Island beachgoers, circa 1910s

Coney Island actually was an island once, separated from Brooklyn by a series of tidal flats and a small stream called Coney Island Creek. Plans to widen the creek to create a shipping canal never came to fruition, and the area was filled in to accommodate the Belt Parkway in the 1930s.

The first hotel on Coney Island was built in 1829, but it wasn't until after the Civil War that the area became popular as a resort, especially for New Yorkers seeking to beat the city heat for a day. Soon bathhouses, hotels, and restaurants were springing up all over the island. Most notable of these was the Manhattan Beach Hotel, which featured lavish ocean-front grounds and plush rooms, shops, and ballrooms. Extravagant fireworks depicting landscapes, battles, and legends were a regular element of an evening's entertainment at the Manhattan Beach Hotel. Of course, not all the hotels were so elegant. The Elephant Hotel, opened in 1885, was actually shaped like an elephant; the head faced the ocean, and visitors could look out through the elephant's "eyes" to view the sea.

The entertainment wasn't always wholesome, either. Aside from the amusement parks, horse racing, and beach fun, Coney

Luna Park, Coney Island, circa 1910s

Coney Island beachgoers

Island also teemed with hustlers pushing prostitution and sucker's games like three-card monte. But these seedier aspects didn't prevent people from coming, any more than fatal accidents on various rides and frequent fires kept the throngs away. From the turn of the twentieth century to the 1950s, millions of people spent their summer days at Coney Island.

Little of the original Coney Island remains today, and as they have since the 1840s, amusement interests are still fighting with developers bent on building residential properties. KeySpan Park, home of the Brooklyn Cyclones minor league baseball team, has helped revitalize the amusement side of Coney Island, and one of the original amusement parks, Astroland, was revived for a time (although it has been involved in a battle with a developer that hadn't been resolved at this writing). The New York Aquarium is undergoing significant renovations, and the annual Nathan's Famous hot dog–eating contest, held every Fourth of July since before World War I, now gets international television coverage. But city officials and developers have yet to agree on a redevelopment plan to adequately address the neighborhood's housing needs while preserving Coney Island's status as a national playground.

Astroland, Coney Island

Street food vendors, Broad Street, 1906

Street food vendors, 50th Street

A TASTE OF NEW YORK

When it comes to New York foods, iconic American fare goes far beyond Brooklyn-style pizza and Coney Island hot dogs. Early Dutch settlers introduced *koolsla* (a salad of shredded cabbage, originally served hot, that survives today as coleslaw) as well as waffles and *olykoecks*, or doughnuts.

Potato chips were invented in a fit of pique by Chef George Crum at Moon's Lake House in Saratoga Springs in 1853 when a diner (who may or may not have been Cornelius Vanderbilt) complained that his fried potatoes were too thick and not crispy enough. Annoyed by the criticism, Crum sliced the potatoes as thin as he could, salted them copiously, and fried them to a delicate crunch, supposedly saying, "Let him try to eat these." The chips were such a hit that they were soon added to the Moon's Lake House menu, and Crum featured them as "Saratoga Chips" when he opened his own restaurant later.

The English muffin was invented in New York City by Samuel Bath Thomas, an English immigrant who in 1880 opened his own bakery in what is now known as Chelsea. He marketed his muffin as a "toaster crumpet," flatter than a traditional crumpet and meant to be split to facilitate toasting. The creation caught on big at New York City hotels, and Thomas soon opened a second building, which today is a co-op apartment building known as "The Muffin Building."

Jell-O had its origins in LeRoy, between Rochester and Buffalo, in the late nineteenth century. A carpenter named Pearle Wait came up with the dessert when he was experimenting with gelatin, and his wife dubbed the fruit-flavored concoction Jell-O. With no capital to market his product, Wait sold the formula for $450, and eventually a businessman named Orator Woodward added Jell-O to his line of products. It was manufactured in LeRoy until 1964; today, it's made in a Kraft/General Foods facility in Delaware. But the little town still celebrates its most famous creation with a museum and Jell-O-themed events.

Jell-O

Anchor Bar, Buffalo

Thousand Island salad dressing was born in Clayton, a resort village on the St. Lawrence Seaway. A fishing guide and his wife served "shore dinners" to their clients, featuring an unusual salad dressing. The dressing caught the fancy of actress May Irwin, who got the recipe from the guide, dubbed it "Thousand Island dressing," and passed the recipe along to George C. Boldt, owner of the Waldorf-Astoria Hotel in New York City. Boldt directed his maitre d'hotel, Oscar Tschirky, to add the dressing to the menu, and thus Tschirky got credit for introducing Thousand Island dressing to the world.

And, of course, the now-ubiquitous Buffalo wings were born at the Anchor Bar in Buffalo in 1964. One Friday night, to feed her son's ravenous friends, Teressa Bellissimo deep-fried some chicken wings—a part that was normally used to make soup stock—and coated them in a tangy sauce. They were such a hit that they were added to the menu almost immediately, and soon other restaurants around the country were making their own versions of Buffalo chicken wings. Today, the Anchor Bar is a destination in its own right, loudly proclaiming its status as the home of the original Buffalo wing and serving more than 1,000 pounds of wings a day.

Long Island

Point Neck, Long Island, 1912

Beaches at Montauk

In some ways, Long Island is a microcosm of New York State (though geographically in reverse). Brooklyn and Queens take up the western end of the island and are part of New York City. As you move east, you encounter first the sprawling suburbs of a major metropolis, and then you're out in the country, surrounded by farms, orchards, world-famous wineries, the Hamptons, and the beach. Parks, public beaches, arts and cultural activities, high-tech firms, farmer's markets, excellent schools, golf courses, even Indian reservations—you can find pretty much whatever you're looking for somewhere on Long Island.

The Dutch settled the areas now known as Brooklyn and Queens, while English Puritan settlers from Connecticut established a community at Southold in 1640. During the Revolutionary War, the British captured the island and maintained it as a stronghold for the duration of the war. The loyalties of those living on the island were divided, with Tory sentiments stronger on the western half and rebel sympathies stronger in the east and north.

The island remained largely rural until after World War II, when the postwar building boom attracted city dwellers anxious to move to the suburbs and G.I.s returning from war and ready to start families. Various parks also fueled the island's tourism industry, which still thrives today. Visitors flock to the beaches and parks during the summer and plan trips to the wineries, fishing villages, and quaint towns of the North Fork, or outings for golf, horseback riding, boating, surfing, or elegant dining on the South Fork.

Postcard view of sand dunes, East Hampton

"Walking dunes," near Montauk

Fishing boat in Montauk Channel

Tannersville and Haines Falls, Catskill Mountains, 1898

THE CATSKILLS

Whoever has made a voyage up the Hudson must remember the Catskill Mountains . . . swelling up to a noble height, and lording it over the surrounding country. . . . When the weather is fair and settled, they are clothed in blue and purple, and print their bold outlines on the clear evening sky; but sometimes, when the rest of the landscape is cloudless, they will gather a hood of gray vapors about their summits, which, in the last rays of the setting sun, will glow and light up like a crown of glory.

So begins Washington Irving's "Rip Van Winkle," and though the description was written nearly two hundred years ago, it remains apt today. The communities tucked among the Catskills have ridden the highs and lows of fickle economics for more than two centuries, but the mountains themselves still lord it over the surrounding country, seemingly unaffected by the puny interests of humans.

Settling this rugged countryside was no easy task. The Native Americans of the region used it for hunting and travel, but chose to establish their villages in areas where farming was easier. Likewise, European explorers and settlers scarcely left an imprint here until well into the eighteenth century.

While nature itself kept most development at bay for many decades, the mountains and forests of the Catskills first received state protection with the establishment of Catskill Park in 1885. In 1894, the state constitution was amended to ensure that the lands would remain "forever wild." Today, the public and private lands within Catskill Park encompass some 700,000 acres, about 300,000 acres of which are state-owned as part of the Catskill Forest Preserve.

Haines Falls, Catskill Mountains, 1870

Sunset Rock, overlooking North and South Lake campground, Catskill Mountains

On the cultural front, the Catskills came into their own in the first half of the twentieth century, after a Yiddish theater star opened an entertainment complex catering to Jewish vacationers. The region quickly became "The Borscht Belt," referring to the beet soup popular among Eastern European immigrants. Hotels, summer camps, bungalow communities, and boarding houses sprouted up throughout the region. Several famous comedians—among them Woody Allen, Mel Brooks, George Burns, and Jerry Lewis—either got their start or performed regularly here in the 1940s, '50s, and '60s.

As air travel and air conditioning became more common after World War II, the Borscht Belt lost much of its cache as a summer destination. The entertainers stopped coming, the fancy resorts closed, and residents, unable to find work locally, moved to other, more economically viable places. Until 2006, the last big entertainment gig in the Catskills was 1969's Woodstock Music and Art Fair.

A few of the big resorts remain, and developers have touted numerous plans for making the Catskills a vacation destination and entertainment center again. On a smaller scale, many of the communities here have gone quietly about the business of building and solidifying their economies from within. The Bethel Woods Center for the Arts opened on the Woodstock site in 2006 and has hosted the New York Philharmonic and a jazz festival that featured the likes of Wynton Marsalis and Dianna Reeves. Sullivan County in particular is benefiting from economic diversification, with a business base that includes finance and insurance companies, warehouse distribution centers, and small high-tech firms.

Kaaterskill Falls, Catskill Mountains

"In the Catskills," 1877 lithograph

Main Street, village of Fleischmanns, Delaware County

WASHINGTON IRVING

Sunnyside, with period re-enactor, Tarrytown

The first American to make his living solely from writing, Washington Irving is credited with coining two still-popular terms for New York City and its residents: Gotham and Knickerbockers, respectively. The latter came from Irving's 1809 spoof, "A History of New York from the Beginning of the World to the End of the Dutch Dynasty," which he published under the pen name Diedrich Knickerbocker. Eventually, the name "Knickerbocker" came to mean anyone from the city, and it's still in use today as the name of New York's professional basketball team, the Knicks.

After several years traveling abroad, Irving returned to New York in 1832 and settled in Tarrytown, now officially called Sleepy Hollow after one of Irving's most famous short stories. Unmarried and childless, he shared his home, called Sunnyside, with his brother and his brother's five daughters and the myriad artists, writers, and politicians who visited him until his death in 1859. He was buried in the cemetery at the Old Dutch Church in Sleepy Hollow.

Sunnyside on the Hudson, Currier and Ives lithograph, late 1800s

Sunnyside still stands, and guides dressed in period clothing tell visitors of Irving's life and writings during tours of the place Irving himself called "a beautiful spot, capable of being made a little paradise."

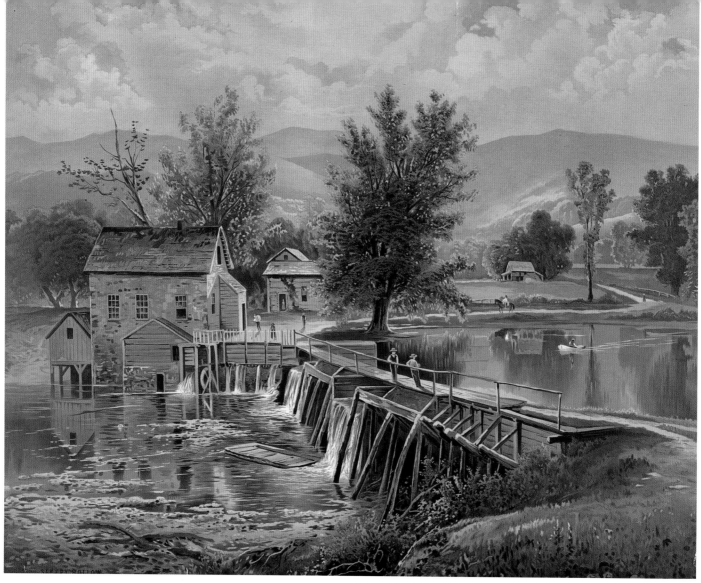

Mill at Sleepy Hollow, 1884

SLEEPY HOLLOW

Sleepy Hollow is the home of arguably the most famous ghost story in American history: "The Galloping Hessian of the Hollow," or, more familiarly, "The Headless Horseman." Washington Irving's short story, *The Legend of Sleepy Hollow*, is set about thirty years after the Revolutionary War in the idyllic countryside where the Hudson River meets the Pocantico River in present-day Westchester County.

Long before the Revolution, though, Dutch trappers and settlers had established trade relationships with the Native Americans of the area. In the 1600s, the Dutch government granted title to a vast swath of land to Frederick Philipse, a Dutch merchant who emigrated to what was then New Amsterdam in 1647. When England took control of the colony in 1664, Philipse swore his loyalty to the British Crown and was rewarded with a royal patent for a large chunk of Westchester County, to be known as Philipse Manor or Philipsburg Manor.

Philipse built a mansion, a dam, a mill, and a church, and he brought in Dutch families to settle nearby, establishing an American version of the Old World's feudal system. Settlers—not only Dutch, but also English, French, and German—paid rent to the Philipse family for the lands they farmed and brought their grain to the Philipse mill, where it was processed and shipped to the West Indies and other markets.

Mill at Philipsburg Manor, Sleepy Hollow

Kykuit estate grounds, with view of Hudson River, Sleepy Hollow

After the Revolution, the residents became landowners themselves in the peaceful agrarian world Irving wrote about. But Sleepy Hollow could not stay unchanged forever. Commerce and industry moved inexorably up the Hudson from Manhattan. First an aqueduct at Croton and later the Hudson River railroad brought laborers and their families to the area, and by the twentieth century, factories began replacing farms as the principal sources of employment.

For most of the twentieth century, the hamlets of Sleepy Hollow and nearby Beekmantown were incorporated as one village called North Tarrytown. In 1997, the village officially changed its name to Sleepy Hollow. Not only does the name make it easier for literary buffs and ghost-hunting enthusiasts to locate, but it provides a unique hook for marketing a variety of attractions to tourists.

There is plenty for today's visitor to explore. Aside from Philipsburg Manor, with its restored grist mill and fully furnished colonial house, Sleepy Hollow also boasts Kykuit, the Rockefeller family estate; an historic lighthouse; and stained glass windows by Marc Chagall and Henri Matisse in the Rockefeller-financed Union Church of Pocantico Hills.

For the outdoors enthusiast, there are the Rockefeller State Preserve, an oasis of meadows, wetlands, and woods adjacent to Kykuit, and Kingsland Point Park, a recreation area on the banks of the Hudson. And for those who secretly yearn for a glimpse of the Headless Horseman, there is the Old Croton Aqueduct Trailway, which passes behind the Old Dutch Church cemetery and crosses the Pocantico River at nearly the exact spot where Ichabod Crane had his terrifying encounter.

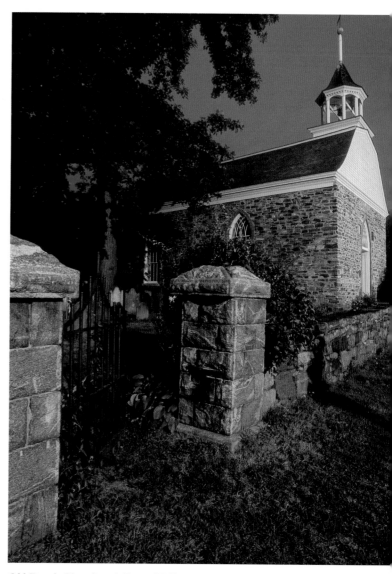

Old Dutch Church and Sleepy Hollow Cemetery

BEAR MOUNTAIN

Settlement and development along the Hudson River in the nineteenth century threatened much of the region's natural beauty. Efforts to establish a park or preserve here were unsuccessful, until state officials announced, in 1908, a plan to relocate the infamous Sing Sing prison to Bear Mountain, so called because the profile of the mountain can be fancied to resemble a snoozing bear. That proposal prompted a group of wealthy businessmen—all of whom had luxurious homes in the area and didn't want their property values degraded by the presence of a prison—to donate land and money to buy up other parcels for preservation. Bear Mountain–Harriman State Park (named for Union Pacific railroad president E. W. Harriman, who led the businessmen's efforts) was established in 1910, and within four years, the park was attracting more than a million visitors a year.

The beginning of the Appalachian Trail, which was constructed in sections by regional organizations and then connected as a continuous trail, is at Bear Mountain. It opened in 1923 and provided a model for other sections of the trail. The park also benefited substantially from Franklin Roosevelt's New Deal programs. The Civil Works Administration and Work Progress Administration spent five years building improvements throughout the park in the 1930s.

Bear Mountain also is home to what, at the time, was the world's longest suspension bridge, which was completed in less

Postcard view of Bear Mountain State Park and bridge, circa 1920s

than two years and without a single fatality. In the 1920s, the Bear Mountain Bridge set new engineering standards for bridges and served as a pattern for building big bridges throughout the Hudson Valley and New York City.

Bear Mountain State Park is just as popular today as it was back when it was newly minted. More people visit Bear Mountain than Yellowstone, partaking of the plethora of outdoor activities available year-round, from boating, hiking, and swimming to sledding, ice skating, and cross-country skiing. Among the attractions are museums, a zoo, and a merry-go-round with hand-carved seats depicting local fauna and hand-painted vistas of the park itself.

Pedestrian path at Hessian Lake, Bear Mountain State Park

View of Bear Mountain State Park and bridge

View of West Point from Constitution Island, circa 1820

WEST POINT

George Washington believed that West Point was the most important strategic place in the colonies. With its location overlooking the Hudson, Washington felt whoever controlled West Point could control traffic on the river. In 1778, he commissioned Thaddeus Kosciuszko, a hero from the Battle of Saratoga, to design a fort that could withstand any attack and provide security for this important water route. American forces built forts and batteries at West Point and extended a 150-ton iron chain across the Hudson to control river traffic. Washington established his headquarters here in 1779, and the fort was never captured by the British.

In 1802, President Thomas Jefferson established the U.S. Military Academy at West Point. The institution was designed to teach the art and science of warfare, with an emphasis on civil engineering. Jefferson and those in charge at West Point recognized that the new and growing country needed to produce its own engineers and designers, instead of relying on foreign powers for these skills. During the first half of the nineteenth century, West Point graduates were responsible for much of the construction of the country's railroads, bridges, roads, and harbors.

Today, the Academy offers a much wider curriculum, awarding bachelor of science degrees in fields ranging from medicine and other sciences to the humanities. Graduates are commissioned as second lieutenants in the U.S. Army and are required to serve at least five years of active duty after

View of West Point from Cold Spring area

graduation. Entry into the Academy is extraordinarily competitive; candidates for one of the 4,000 slots have to be recommended by a member of Congress or the Army, and they must meet stringent physical, academic, and leadership requirements.

West Point instructors are fond of noting that "much of the history we teach was made by people we taught." Indeed, the list of graduates is an impressive one, peppered with familiar names from history books: Ulysses S. Grant and Robert E. Lee, George Patton and Douglas MacArthur, Dwight Eisenhower and Norman Schwarzkopf. Astronaut Buzz Aldrin, who was part of the first manned landing on the moon, graduated from West Point in 1951. Kristin Baker, the first woman Brigade commander for the U.S. Corps of Cadets, graduated in 1990.

Cadets at attention, U.S. Military Academy, 1889

Cadets at attention, U.S. Military Academy, 1889

Cadets at Alumni Review, U.S. Military Academy, 2006

THE HUDSON VALLEY

In 1609, the Dutch hired English explorer Henry Hudson to find a quick sea route to China. Hudson's explorations brought him to New York Bay and then up the river that the Mahicans called "the river that flows both ways." Hudson traveled on his ship, the *Half Moon*, nearly as far as present-day Albany. He was forced to turn around when the river became too shallow to navigate. He had to admit he had not yet found an all-water route from the Atlantic to the Pacific. But the Dutch knew he had found a rich resource for commercial activity, and it didn't take them long to build a trading post just south of present-day Albany.

During the middle of the eighteenth century, the Hudson Valley was a British stronghold and a major defense against a possible French invasion from Canada during the French and Indian War. The region also saw much action during the Revolutionary War, when the British tried to squash the American rebellion by cutting New England off from the rest of the colonies.

The Erie Canal brought a new era of prosperity to the communities along the Hudson Valley. For the first time, there was a cheap and easy way to ship goods from New York City to the Great Lakes and vice versa. Industry thrived along the Hudson until the mid-twentieth century.

Drawn by the area's beauty as well as its proximity to New York City, several wealthy industrialists and prominent citizens built grand estates along the banks of the river during the nineteenth century. Some of the most notable homes that still stand include the Gothic-revival Lyndhurst, just south of Tarrytown, built in 1838 and designed by renowned architect Alexander Jackson Davis; the palatial Vanderbilt mansion in Hyde Park, completed in 1898; Montgomery Place, a 434-acre property with a home designed by Alexander Jackson Davis and a landscape by Andrew Jackson Downing; and Frederic Church's Moorish-style Olana, near the city of Hudson.

Henry Hudson's Half Moon *in 1609, lithograph dated 1909*

Replica of the Half Moon *in the Hudson Highlands*

Hudson River scenery, viewed from Bear Mountain Bridge

Known as America's Rhine for its awe-inspiring natural beauty, the Hudson River has been named an American Heritage River, and a portion of the eastern bank is designated as a National Historic Landmark. As industry declined along the river, the Hudson Valley was reborn as a residential haven for people seeking to escape the costs and crowds of city living. Today's residents work hard to balance the expectations of modern suburbanites with the desire to protect the valley's rural character.

"Hudson River Scenery," 1878 lithograph

Watercolor view of the Hudson Highlands from Newburgh, 1846

Just as the vast American wilderness touched the basest chords in the souls of the European traders and land speculators who first arrived here, it also provided inspiration for nineteenth-century artists. Thomas Cole argued that America, a new country in the New World, cried out for a new artistic aesthetic, one that broke from the European aesthetic the same way the colonies broke from British rule. Cole's grand landscapes and skillful uses of atmospheric lighting earned him the title of founder of the Hudson River School of painting.

In his own works and those of others of the period, mankind is dwarfed by the magnificence of nature, achieving true significance only through the divine spark of self-awareness. Many of the paintings incorporate dead or broken tree stumps, one of the school's best-known symbols for the fleetingness and fragility of life.

By the end of the nineteenth century, Hudson River School paintings were considered rather ho-hum and old-fashioned, especially in light of the Industrial Revolution. They enjoyed a spike in popularity after World War I, when war-weary Americans longed for simpler times and wished to be reminded of the breadth, promise, and peace of their great country. In the 1960s and '70s, these paintings again took on a moral message of being in sympathy with the environment and thereby in touch with God. Today, Hudson River School art is valued for its contribution to the development of uniquely American artistic sensibilities as well as for the many layers of meaning it has represented over the years.

The river itself also had many ups and downs in its health. As industry grew in river towns in the late-nineteenth and early-twentieth centuries, raw sewage and industrial waste polluted the waters. Even today, fishermen along the Upper Hudson can only do catch-and-release fishing; levels of PCBs and other toxins are too high to allow for safe consumption of fish from those waters. Clean-up efforts over the past several decades have made the Lower Hudson (actually an estuary of the Atlantic Ocean) safe for aquatic life again, and after decades of litigation, clean-up of the Upper Hudson is set to begin in earnest in 2009—just in time for the quadricentennial celebrations of Henry Hudson's 1609 voyage.

View of the Hudson Highlands from Crows Nest

Artist painting Hudson Valley scenery near Tarrytown

Sunset over the Hudson River in Columbia County

PRESIDENTIAL PALACES

New York has been home to four presidents: Martin Van Buren, Millard Fillmore, Theodore Roosevelt, and Franklin Delano Roosevelt. It is also the adopted home of former President Bill Clinton and New York Senator and 2008 Democratic presidential hopeful Hillary Clinton.

Van Buren, the eighth U.S. president and the first to be born as an American citizen, was born in Kinderhook in Columbia County. In 1839, while serving as president, he bought an estate there, which he named Lindenwald. After he left the White House, he managed the estate as a profitable working farm. Much of the land around the mansion, now the Martin Van Buren National Historic Site, is a conservation area, and the surroundings give visitors a realistic impression of Lindenwald's atmosphere when Van Buren was an elder statesman here.

The Millard Fillmore House, in Cayuga County in north-central New York, is much less imposing and has been altered greatly since Fillmore built it in 1826. Fillmore lived in the simple frame house for only four years before moving to Buffalo. The home has since been moved, added onto, allowed to deteriorate, and refurbished many times over. Still, it is the only extant home, other than the White House, that has significant associations with the thirteenth U.S. president.

Springwood, FDR's estate at Hyde Park, may be the best-known of New York's presidential residences. He grew up here, educated by tutors and governesses, in a rural cocoon removed from the rapid changes of the Industrial Revolution. As governor of New York and later as president, he often sought the peace and seclusion of his childhood home. In 1944, when he was gravely ill and worn out from World War II, Roosevelt said, "All that is within me cries out to go back to my home on the Hudson River."

FDR's cousin Theodore, a Manhattanite who preceded him in both the governor's mansion and the White House, felt much the same way about Oyster Bay, Long Island, which he discovered on family vacations when he was a boy in the 1870s. An avid outdoorsman, Teddy Roosevelt loved hiking, riding, swimming, and rowing at Oyster Bay. When he and his wife Alice were starting their family, he felt that Oyster Bay was the best possible place to settle down. He nearly halted construction of the house, called Sagamore Hill, when Alice died after giving birth to their

Lindenwald, Martin Van Buren National Historic Site, Kinderhook, 1937

daughter, but was convinced to go ahead. After he remarried, he and second wife Edith raised six children in the Queen Anne–style home, and both died there.

In 1999, just before leaving the White House, Bill and Hillary Clinton bought a $1.7 million, 100-year-old Dutch colonial home in quiet, tony Chappaqua, just outside New York City. The following year, Hillary Clinton ran for and won her first term as U.S. senator. She handily won re-election in 2006 and, in 2008, launched an historic campaign for president. As presidential palaces go, the Clintons' five-bedroom in Chappaqua is positively modest, situated close to both the road and the house next door, but like most presidential homes, it does have a romantic name: In Chappaqua history, the property is known as Little Brook Farm.

Interior room at Lindenwald, Martin Van Buren National Historic Site, Kinderhook

Springwood, Hyde Park, July 1941

Springwood, Hyde Park

KINGSTON

Senate House, Kingston, 1777

residents hold a re-enactment of the burning of the city every other year (although they don't actually burn the buildings). The Rondout, as it's called today, is Kingston's downtown district, an artists' community filled with galleries, museums, and performance spaces. The annual Kingston Jazz Festival is held here, as is the Artists' Soapbox Derby, a unique combination of traditional soapbox racing and kinetic-sculpture competition that draws thousands of spectators every year.

Rondout District, Kingston

The first capital of New York, Kingston suffered mightily during the Revolutionary War. After the Battle of Saratoga, British troops burned the city virtually to the ground, including the major granary there and the wheat it processed, which supplied much of the colony at the time. Many of the Kingston militia were still at Saratoga or other forts to the south, and the remaining force stood little chance against the 2,000 British regulars who marched through on their destructive mission.

In 1797, after briefly being located in Poughkeepsie, the capital of New York was established in Albany, and a rebuilt Kingston turned its attentions to commerce and industry. A town called Rondout, now part of Kingston itself, was an important shipping center for coal that came from Pennsylvania into New York, and bluestone—the same kind of stone used to build Stonehenge—was quarried and shipped to New York City for sidewalks. The community also had a cement quarry, brick-making factories, and large ice-warehousing operations on the Hudson.

Today, Kingston celebrates its history in both its uptown (where the original capital was) and Rondout areas. Uptown

RAILROADS

The Empire State Express, *headed southbound along the Hudson River, circa 1940s*

Amtrak passenger train, headed westbound through the Mohawk Valley

The history of railroading in New York is a bewildering mix of mergers, acquisitions, and charters, including numerous rail companies that never laid an inch of track or shipped a single item. The Mohawk and Hudson Railroad, chartered in 1826, was the first permanent railroad in the state, built between Schenectady and Albany to connect the Mohawk and Hudson Rivers. By the middle of the nineteenth century, as many as a dozen additional rail companies were chartered in the state, and in 1853, ten of them merged to form the New York Central Railroad, effectively connecting Albany and Buffalo by rail. Additional growth and consolidation followed, the most significant of which was the acquisition and subsequent merger of the Hudson River Railroad and the New York Central by Cornelius Vanderbilt in the 1860s. Known as the "Water Level Route," the New York Central mainline ran north along the Hudson River and east along the Erie Canal and the Lake Erie shoreline.

During its illustrious history, the New York Central operated such legendary passenger trains as the *Empire State Express*, which was the first high-speed train and ran from 1891 to 1971, and the *20th Century Limited*, a celebrated express train that traveled between New York City and Chicago. As the railroad industry fell on hard times in the 1960s, the New York Central merged with the rival Pennsylvania Railroad to form the Penn Central, which was ultimately bailed out by the federal government with the creation of Conrail in 1976. Today, most of the New York Central's old lines are operated by CSX.

Freight trains still transport goods across the Empire State, and passenger trains, primarily Amtrak as well as smaller commuter lines, continue to transport people from New York City to Buffalo and back again, through the Hudson and Mohawk Valleys, and around many regions of the state. Several tourism-related trains are also in operation in New York, notably the Adirondack Railroad, which runs from Utica to the Adirondacks. Especially popular are the leaf-peeping excursions in the fall.

Four New York Central trains at Little Falls, Mohawk Valley, 1890

Albany and the Hudson River, 1850s lithograph

ALBANY

On his exploratory voyage up the river that would be named for him, Henry Hudson was forced to turn around near present-day Albany and head back to New York Harbor; the river was too shallow for him to continue. Still, the river provided an excellent means of transporting furs from the wilderness to New York City and on to Europe, so the Dutch built Fort Orange as a trading post and strategic protection for its shipping route. When the British took control of the colony, they renamed the fort Albany in honor of the Duke of York and Albany. With its location on the Hudson River and its proximity to the shipping routes of the Mohawk Valley, including the Erie Canal and prominent rail lines, the city remained as a prominent shipping and commercial center well into the twentieth century.

Albany has been New York's capital since 1797, and the governor's mansion has housed many notable figures over the years. Four New York governors have gone on to be president of the United States: Martin Van Buren, Grover Cleveland,

Market Street, Albany, 1805

Theodore Roosevelt, and Franklin Delano Roosevelt. Van Buren and Theodore Roosevelt also served as vice president, as did four of their gubernatorial brethren. Six other governors launched unsuccessful presidential campaigns, including Samuel Tilden, who won the popular vote in 1876 but lost the electoral college in a highly controversial election against Republican Rutherford

Albany waterfront, 1890

Replica of Henry Hudson's Half Moon *ship, Albany waterfront*

Albany skyline

Below: *Albany skyline, 1911*

Empire Plaza and The Egg

B. Hayes; Al Smith, who in 1928 became the first Roman Catholic major-party nominee but lost to Herbert Hoover in a landslide; and Thomas Dewey, whom the *Chicago Daily Tribune* famously misidentified as the winner in the 1948 contest between Dewey and Harry S Truman. Two New York governors, John Jay and Charles Evans Hughes, became Chief Justices of the United States Supreme Court. William H. Seward, Hamilton Fish, and Hughes served as the U.S. secretary of state.

New York made history in its leadership again in 2008 when Governor Eliot Spitzer resigned following revelations about his use of a high-priced prostitution service. On March 17, his lieutenant governor, David Paterson, took over as governor, becoming only the third black governor in the United States since Reconstruction and the first to hold the office in New York. Paterson also is the first legally blind person to assume the governorship.

Scandals notwithstanding, much of Albany's economy revolves around the state government. Those who don't work for legislators or state agencies are employed primarily by universities, high-tech firms, or other private corporations. The University at Albany's nanotechnology program has positioned Albany as a national leader in this field and as the anchor of a nineteen-county area of the state branded as "Tech Valley."

The city also has a vibrant arts and culture community. The New York State Museum is headquartered here, and national and international acts perform in the massive Times Union Center (formerly the Pepsi Arena) and The Egg, a midsized venue located in the Empire Plaza at the center of state government operations. Lark Street is sometimes referred to as "Albany's Greenwich Village" for its collection of coffee shops, art galleries, antique stores, and bars.

View of Albany skyline and capitol building

Postcard view of Albany and capitol building

Birdseye view of Troy, 1909

TROY

Man dressed as Uncle Sam for annual Victorian Stroll, 2006

Troy bills itself as the home of Uncle Sam. According to legend, a local butcher named Samuel Wilson supplied the military during the War of 1812, stamping his barrels of meat with "U.S." Soldiers familiar with Wilson jokingly referred to the supplies as coming from "Uncle Sam." Sam Wilson is buried in the Oakwood Cemetery, and every September, near Wilson's birthday, the city holds an Uncle Sam Parade to celebrate this famous resident.

Not that there is any shortage of Trojans to honor. Hannah Lord Montague, who wearied of washing her husband's shirts when only the collar and cuffs were dirty, invented detachable collars and cuffs. This innovation not only changed men's fashion for nearly a century but also created an entirely new industry. Today's "Arrow" shirts, made by Cluett, Peabody and Company, originated with Hannah Lord Montague's patented idea. Shirt manufacturing was done mainly by women, and Troy resident Kate Mullany organized the nation's first female labor union, the Collar Laundry Union. The union went on strike in 1864 and within six days won a 25 percent increase in wages. Mullany went on to become second vice president of the National Labor Union. Her home in Troy is a National Historic Landmark.

In 1823, the *Troy Sentinel* first published the Christmas poem "A Visit from St. Nicholas," known to many today by its famous first line: "'Twas the night before Christmas, and all through the house. . . ." The poem was published anonymously, and there is some debate over who the author was. It was long believed to be the work of Clement Clarke Moore, but some people now think it was written by Henry Livingston Jr., a Poughkeepsie poet whose quiet life was overshadowed by his more famous brothers, the

Birdseye view of Troy

theologian Rev. John Henry Livingston and the politically minded Gilbert Livingston.

During Prohibition and up through World War II, Troy had a reputation as a city of vice. Speakeasies and brothels operated fairly openly in the 1920s and '30s, and gangsters such as the infamous Legs Diamond bootlegged freely in the city. Mame Fay, one of the wealthiest women in Troy, operated a famous bordello on Sixth Avenue from around the turn of the century until 1941. When she died in 1943, Fay's estate was valued at the equivalent of about $3.5 million.

Today, Troy has a thriving antique district downtown and is home to several art galleries, cafes, and shops. The weekly Farmer's Market—held outdoors during the summer and indoors during the winter—is a popular attraction for locals and visitors alike. Rensselaer Polytechnic Institute, the oldest technological institute in the English-speaking world, attracts college students from around the world. A plethora of parades, festivals, and special events keeps Troy's citizens and visitors busy year-round.

Shirt factory, Troy, 1907

Saratoga Springs, Currier and Ives lithograph, circa 1870s

Broadway, Saratoga Springs

SARATOGA SPRINGS

The Iroquois Indians—most likely Mohawk—called this area *Sarachtogue* and prized both the quality of the furs (made thick and shiny by the saline and minerals in the local water) and the healing properties they believed the mineral springs possessed. Mohawk friends of Sir William Johnson, the British superintendent of Indian affairs and a hero of the French and Indian War, brought him here to treat war wounds in the spring now known as High Rock Spring, which is still open to visitors today.

In the nineteenth century, Saratoga Springs attracted wealthy visitors anxious to "take the waters" in the mineral bathhouses that had been built to exploit the supposed medicinal powers of the springs. The opening of the Saratoga Springs Race Course in 1863 added to the village's attraction; the race course drew record crowds at its inaugural event.

The rich and powerful were common visitors during the village's heyday. Members of the elite Rockefeller, Vanderbilt, and Whitney families frequented Saratoga Springs, as did such luminaries as J. P. Morgan, Andrew Jackson, and Diamond Jim Brady.

Unlike many of the state's nineteenth-century hot spots, Saratoga Springs has lost none of its status as a must-see destination over the years. The Saratoga Performing Arts Center (called SPAC, to rhyme with "track," by locals) is a major concert venue for national and international acts, as well as the site of an annual Native American festival and the summer home of both the

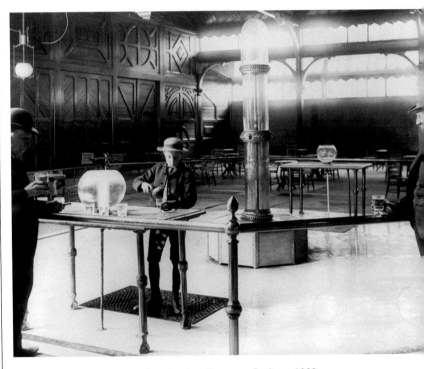

Boy serving water at natural spring bar, Saratoga Springs, 1889

New York City Ballet and the Philadelphia Orchestra. Its Caffe Lena has hosted music legends Bob Dylan and Arlo Guthrie, and Yaddo, a 400-acre artists' community next to the Saratoga Springs Race Course, has hosted a Nobel Prize winner and sixty Pulitzer Prize winners.

Saratoga Springs Race Course, 1913

Saratoga Springs Race Course

LAKE CHAMPLAIN

"M'Donough's victy. on Lake Champlain," Currier and Ives lithograph, 1846

Sailboats moored near Valcour Island

In 1609, while Henry Hudson was exploring the river that ended in New York Harbor, looking for a northwest passage to India, French explorer Samuel de Champlain was seeking that same fabled passage from points further north. He encountered the lake that later was named for him and, in doing so, charted an easily traveled route from the St. Lawrence River to the Hudson Valley. Even in winter, it was easier to transport furs and other supplies on sleds over the ice-covered lake than to take the sloppy, unpaved roads of the time.

The lake was a significant commercial and military asset in the eighteenth and nineteenth centuries, sharing a shoreline with Vermont, New York, and Quebec. Several forts and railroad crossings were built to protect water rights and facilitate trade. During the War of 1812, the American fleet led by Captain Thomas Macdonough secured a pivotal victory over the superior British Royal Navy and helped to thwart the invading British.

Today, the lake's role in commerce and trade is practically nonexistent, and the once-important ports of Plattsburgh and Port Henry on the New York side and Burlington on the Vermont shore see little traffic save for ferries, lake cruise ships, and recreational boaters. The landscape around Lake Champlain remains largely undeveloped, thanks to an enduring conservation and preservation mentality that took root early in the nineteenth century. Biking and hiking are popular land-based activities, as is watching the water for a glimpse of Champ, Lake Champlain's version of the Loch Ness monster. If you don't see Champ in the lake, you can settle for its image on a T-shirt, coffee mug, or other souvenir.

Vacationers at Lake Champlain, 1890

Below: *Swimming on Lake Champlain*

"Montcalm Trying to Stop the Massacre," Battle of Fort William Henry, 1757, lithograph circa 1870

DEFENDING LAND AND SEA

Lake Champlain and nearby Lake George were critical to the movement of furs and other goods in the New World, and almost from the moment of their discovery various European powers fought for control of these strategic waterways. The British built Fort William Henry on the southern end of Lake George to protect against French encroachment from the north; this fort was in operation for only two years but was immortalized in James Fenimore Cooper's *The Last of the Mohicans*. Numerous movies have portrayed a vicious slaughter of English soldiers after the fort's surrender to the French, but most historians believe those accounts were greatly fictionalized, noting that Indians knew the Europeans would pay more for soldiers returned alive and probably only assaulted soldiers to take their clothing, weapons, or other booty as payment for their services to the French. Today, a reconstruction of Fort William Henry stands on the original's site, and markers and monuments recount the fort's short but tumultuous history.

Further north, on the narrow strip of land between Lake George and Lake Champlain, the French had built Fort Carillon, from which they launched the devastating attack against Fort William Henry. In 1758, the year after Fort William Henry fell, the British amassed a huge army to take Fort Carillon, but the French withstood the siege, handing Britain a humiliating defeat. The British tried again the following year and this time succeeded, and British General Amherst renamed the fort Ticonderoga.

Nearly twenty years later, Ticonderoga would be the site of the first major American victory in the Revolutionary War: The Green Mountain Boys, led by Ethan Allen and Benedict Arnold, crossed Lake Champlain from Vermont one night in May 1775 and surprised the sleeping British, who only had a half garrison manning the fort. As an American stronghold for the next two years, Fort Ticonderoga was a critical staging area for the colonial army.

In the 1820s, William Ferris Pell purchased the fort and surrounding grounds and built a hotel for tourists who came to visit the ruins. Restoration of the fort began in the next century, and since 1931 it has been managed as an educational historic site by the Fort Ticonderoga Association. Some 90,000 people a year visit the site. Visitors can enjoy self-guided tours, watch the daily musket-firing demonstrations, or wander through the museum.

Still further north are the remains of Crown Point, originally built by the French in the 1750s at the height of the conflict between Great Britain and France over claims to the New World. The British tried and failed four times to take over what the French had named Fort St. Frederic; they didn't take actual possession of the site until 1759, and only after the French abandoned it. British fortifications helped them defeat the French in Canada. American forces captured Crown Point and, importantly, its cannons and other ordnance, in 1775, but the British regained control two years later and kept it throughout the duration of the war. New York acquired the site in 1910 and opened it to the public. Visitors today can learn about Crown Point's history through exhibits in the visitors center and stroll around the ruins of the French-British-American fort.

Guns on bastion, restored Fort Ticonderoga, 1935

Guns on bastion, restored Fort Ticonderoga

Left: *French and Indian War battle re-enactment, Fort Ticonderoga*

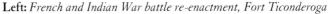

View from Bald Mountain, 1911

THE ADIRONDACKS

The Adirondack Park may be the only park in the United States that is constitutionally protected from development. The need to protect the Adirondack region—especially the watershed that supplied the Erie Canal, so vital to New York's economy—was recognized in 1873, when a man named Verplanck Colvin wrote a report recommending preservation of the wilderness region. Twelve years later, as superintendent of New York's state land survey, Colvin created the Adirondack Forest Preserve, which became Adirondack Park in 1892. In the face of intense lobbying by logging and other development interests, environmentalists of the time worked to amend the state constitution and succeeded in adding this clause in 1894: "The lands of the State . . . shall be forever kept as wild forest lands." The "forever wild" clause, as it is known today, prohibits logging and the leasing, selling, or exchanging of state lands. The constitutional amendment is widely viewed as the foundation for the federal National Wilderness Act of 1964, which also seeks to protect wilderness areas from development.

A little over one-third of the six-million-acre park is protected forest land. The rest of it is privately owned but highly regulated by the Adirondack Park Agency, so even those private parcels are subject to severe limits on their development. As a result, the Adirondacks retains much of the character it had when Europeans first identified it on maps only as "Deer Hunting Country." The old-growth forests support an amazing variety of wildlife, including some 260 bird species, as well as deer, black bear, and smaller fauna such as otters and porcupines. The fishing is excellent, thanks in part to regulations that prevent overfishing,

Hiker on Bald Mountain, 1900

and many an avid angler counts the days until he can get up to his favorite stream or river to fish for black bass or trout.

For hikers, the High Peaks—forty-six of the tallest mountains in the Adirondacks collection—are the park's main attraction, and the stunning panoramic views they offer are the prize. For less experienced hikers, there are more than fifty smaller peaks to climb. Because of their rounded tops, the Adirondacks are relatively easy to scale, but some of the mountains don't have established trails, so hikers have to follow game trails or make their own.

View of the High Peaks from Mount Jo

Hikers on the summit of Mount Marcy

Two men and two dogs canoeing in the Adirondacks, 1890

Postcard view of Blue Mountain and Blue Mountain Lake

Fisherman on Lake George

Saw mill and block house at Fort Anne Creek, 1789

Lumber mill, Broome County, 1971

LOGGING AND LUMBER

When European explorers arrived on the northeastern coast of what became the United States, the forests of the New World seemed inexhaustible. Settlers cleared massive areas of land for farming and used the lumber for houses, boats, wagons, and even plank roads to facilitate travel through the often-marshy areas of both Manhattan and Upstate. Paper mills and saw mills established themselves next to rivers and lakes in the forests of the Adirondacks and elsewhere throughout the state, and good lumberjacks never had trouble finding work in New York.

As a result of unregulated logging and aggressive expansion of agriculture and settlements, less than a quarter of the state's land remained as forest by the end of the nineteenth century. The modern conservation movement got its start then as people began to realize that the country's natural resources were not limitless. Theodore Roosevelt's calls for conserving open space and protecting wilderness areas for future generations reinforced the new conservation ethic, especially in New York, where the state constitution contains a "forever wild" clause protecting public lands from development.

The forestry industry remains an important element of New York's economy, employing more than 60,000 people and generating some $4.6 billion in annual revenues. The skills of the forest-related trades are celebrated every August at the New York State Woodsmen's Field Days in Boonville, in the foothills of the Adirondacks. Competitors from as far away as Australia and New Zealand vie in various lumber-related contests in front of thousands of spectators, and exhibitors show off the latest in forestry equipment.

Thanks to public and private conservation efforts, nearly two-thirds of New York is now forest land; the roughly 18.5 million acres of woods is more than existed in the state 300 years ago. Most of the wooded land is privately owned, but all of it provides environmental and recreational benefits, not to mention natural beauty, for New Yorkers and visitors.

Lumberjill National Championship, New York State Woodsmen's Field Days, Boonville, 2005

GREAT CAMPS OF THE ADIRONDACKS

In the years following the Civil War, Americans developed an abiding interest in the outdoors and what we now call "adventure travel." The Adirondacks offered both in full measure, and the 1869 publication of William H. H. Murray's "Adventures in the Wilderness, or Camp-Life in the Adirondacks" spawned a rush of general interest the likes of which the region hadn't seen before. Within a few years, there were more than 200 hotels in the Adirondacks to cater to the tourists who flocked here, looking for a taste of wilderness and adventure. The mountains were crisscrossed with railways and stage-coach lines to accommodate the throngs of visitors.

Among those who wanted to escape to the mountains were the very well-to-do, who built lavish compounds on remote parcels and seemed determined to outdo each other in rustic luxury. A typical great camp is fashioned of local materials—rough-hewn timber, local stone, roots, and branches—and consists of a main building surrounded by smaller structures, which may house guest quarters or recreation centers or be built for other functions. The compound system provided a fine balance between privacy and a sense of community, but there was a more practical aspect, too: Several smaller structures some distance apart from each other reduced the risk of fire devastating an entire camp.

William West Durant built the first of these great camps near Raquette Lake. His idea was to lure wealthy families to his 6,000-acre property to build their own vacation homes on his land. Financial woes forced Durant to sell out to the Vanderbilts, who added citified amenities such as flush toilets, electricity, and hot and cold running water to the Sagamore Camp. The Vanderbilts treated guests to gourmet meals cooked and served by uniformed staff, and offered a range of entertainment that included billiards, tennis, and a two-lane bowling alley, which is still in use today.

The Great Depression brought about the end of the great camp era, and many compounds were razed or allowed to fall into disrepair, leaving only their legends of luxury behind them. Those that survive evoke the romanticism of the late nineteenth and early twentieth centuries.

Sagamore and Camp Pine Knot are National Historic Landmarks, and Sagamore and another great camp, Santanoni, are open to the public during the warmer months.

Raquette Lake Hotel, 1889

Vacationers relaxing on sandy beach, Adirondacks, 1888

Great Camp Sagamore, Raquette Lake

Bowling alley at Great Camp Sagamore

SARANAC LAKE

Tuberculosis made Saranac Lake famous. When Dr. Edward Livingston Trudeau (great-grandfather of "Doonesbury" cartoonist Garry Trudeau) was diagnosed with the then-incurable lung disease in 1874, he followed the conventional wisdom of the time and sought a change of climate at the village of Paul Smiths in the Adirondacks. The fresh air and sunlight restored his health to a remarkable extent, and two years later he moved to Saranac Lake, then little more than a camp village for lumberjacks, outdoors enthusiasts, and their guides, and he set up a medical practice. In 1882, after reading of a Prussian doctor's success in treating tuberculosis with a "rest cure" in the mountains, Trudeau founded the Adirondack Cottage Sanitarium. Unlike large institutions for consumptive patients, "cure cottages" were designed to provide the patient with plenty of fresh air and natural light. Some of the cottages were built for this purpose, while others were converted into cure cottages by adding glass-enclosed "cure porches," where patients would spend their days resting on day beds or reclining chairs. *Treasure Island* author Robert Louis Stevenson sought the rest cure here in 1887, adding to the village's fashionable cache, and the advent of railroad service made the village much more accessible. As word of the rejuvenating properties of the Adirondack air and the village's amenities spread, more famous and powerful people came to take the cure: Mark Twain, Albert Einstein, Jack

Winter Carnival, Saranac Lake, 2004

Dempsey, and Al Jolson, and U.S. presidents Benjamin Harrison, William McKinley, Theodore Roosevelt, and Calvin Coolidge. Between 1880 and 1920, the population of Saranac Lake exploded from about 500 to more than 6,000.

By the 1950s, treatment for tuberculosis was done almost entirely through medication, and the rest cure fell out of vogue. Saranac Lake's focus turned from the ill to family leisure time, and the village capitalized on the amenities and services that had been built to care for consumption patients to attract a new breed of vacationers. One of the most popular attractions yet today is the annual Winter Carnival, which started as a one-day fling in 1898 and now is a weeklong celebration. The oldest winter carnival in the United States, Saranac Lake's festivities include parades, performances, contests, and fireworks, as well as the world-famous Ice Palace. Many of the cure cottages have been preserved and restored, and summer visitors can once again take the train to the village; the Adirondack Scenic Railroad began offering regular runs in 2000.

Winter Carnival, Saranac Lake, 1909

Chapel and cottages, Adirondack Cottage Sanitarium, Saranac Lake, 1906

Robert Louis Stevenson Memorial Cottage, Saranac Lake

LAKE PLACID

Lake Placid is best known as the site of two Winter Olympics, particularly the 1980 "Miracle on Ice" contest, when a group of collegiate and amateur hockey players defeated the Soviet Union's national team on their way to winning the gold medal. Until 1984, when Los Angeles hosted the summer games for the second time, Lake Placid was the only North American venue to host two Olympics contests.

Lake Placid first earned its reputation as a winter getaway in the early 1900s, when Melvil Dewey (inventor of the Dewey Decimal System) kept his Lake Placid Club open through the winter. By the 1920s, it boasted a ski jump and speed skating rink, and by the end of the decade, Olympics officials were convinced that Lake Placid had the best facilities for the 1932 winter games. Village resident Jack Shea was the first person to win two gold medals at the Winter Olympics; he doubled in speed skating in 1932. In 2002, Shea carried the Olympic torch through Lake Placid on its way to the Salt Lake City games. At the 1932 games, a total of 252 athletes participated, as compared to 1,072 participants at the 1980 Lake Placid Olympics.

Aside from its Olympic history, Lake Placid also played an important role in the anti-slavery movement of the 1840s. Abolitionist Gerrit Smith bought a great deal of land here in 1845 and gave large homesteads to his slaves, for all practical purposes reforming the laws governing land ownership without going through the messy process of state legislative approval. Smith's activities attracted the attention of famed abolitionist John Brown, who moved here from Kansas and bought nearly 250 acres for what would be known as the Freed Slave Utopian Experiment. Before Brown was executed for his role in the slave rebellion at Harpers Ferry, Virginia, he asked to be buried on his farm in North Elba, near Lake Placid; the site is both a state and national historic landmark.

Even today, Lake Placid's charms aren't limited to the winter months. Located only thirteen miles from Whiteface Mountain, one of the Adirondacks' High Peaks and the only one accessible by car, the village serves as a convenient base in the summer for hikers. For those who don't hike, there are also golf courses reminiscent of the mountainous courses in Scotland, the annual Ironman Triathlon competition, horse shows, or excellent catch-and-release fly fishing on the Au Sable River.

Poster promoting winter sports at Lake Placid, 1938

Above: *View of Mirror Lake and Lake Placid*

Top: *View of Lake Placid, 1914*

Opening ceremony grounds and eternal flame from 1980 Olympic Games, Lake Placid

A few inches of snow at once can lead many cities and communities to virtually shut down, but Upstaters don't consider snowfall significant unless it can be measured in feet. Syracuse and Buffalo vie each year for the Golden Snowball, a trophy given to the big Upstate city with the highest snowfall. Although Buffalo usually gets the most media attention for its winters, Syracuse has won the trophy every year since 2002, along with a $100 check, which is donated to a school hat-and-mitten drive in the winning city. The other Upstate cities officially in the running for the Golden Snowball are Albany, Binghamton, and Rochester, but they rarely place better than a distant third behind Syracuse and Buffalo.

For the Indians, and later for European trappers and settlers, the typically intense snowfall of Upstate winters presented challenges for hunting and travel. The Indians solved the problem of moving through knee-deep or higher snow with snowshoes. Believed to be in use for more than 6,000 years in Central Asia and brought to the Americas by ancient migrants from that land, the Indians of the heavily forested Northeast adapted the design to suit their terrain. Wood was carved and steamed so it could be bent into an oval, and the frame was laced with rawhide to support the foot. This design had a short tail at the heel and was more maneuverable in the forest than the long-tailed, upswept-toe Yukon design. Walking with snowshoes also kept the hands free for hunting. The French called snowshoes *raquettes* due to their resemblance to tennis rackets, and legend has it that Raquette Lake in the Adirondacks was so named when French trappers saw mounds of snowshoes that area Indians had discarded on the lake's shore.

Until the 1970s or so, most people who snowshoed did so from motives of survival or as a necessary adjunct to employment or transportation. In the past forty years, though, snowshoeing has become a popular winter sport, especially for people who want to leave the groomed ski and snowmobile trails and strike out on their own explorations.

Since no one can control the weather, and many people can't escape to sunnier, warmer locales during the winter months, New Yorkers have come up with ways to have fun with the snow. The "I Love NY" winter activity and travel guide includes five pages of festivals, carnivals, competitions, and other events to help pass the time, ranging from the Winter Carnival in Saranac

Poster promoting winter sports in New York, 1930s

Downhill skiing at Gore Mountain

Lake to Utica's annual Snowfari to the Winter Jazz Festival in New York City—not to mention the smaller winter celebrations hosted by virtually every village in the state. New York is latticed with more than fifty cross-country ski trails, countless snowmobile trails, and nearly fifty centers like Gore Mountain, Whiteface Mountain, Thunder Ridge, and Greek Peak for downhill skiing, snowboarding, and tubing.

Ski jump at Norsemen Interstate Championship Ski Tournament, Tarrytown, circa 1920s

Olympic ski jump, Lake Placid

Snowshoeing near Brant Lake in the Adirondacks

ST. LAWRENCE SEAWAY

In her 1942 memoir, *Our Hearts Were Young and Gay*, Cornelia Otis Skinner recounts running aground on the liner *Montcalm* in the St. Lawrence River some years earlier: "The tide was going rapidly down. . . . The side which was at a lower angle became even more so. . . . The engines were now working themselves into a threatened angina trying to shove us out of the mud." She and a friend were on their way to Europe and eventually secured passage on another ship, but their experience in the early twentieth century was by no means unique. Until the late 1950s, the St. Lawrence was only navigable as far as Montreal; beyond were the Lachine Rapids, virtually impassable by any large vessel. To open the river to large oceangoing vessels required building seven locks and an extensive series of canals.

French explorer Jacques Cartier is credited as the first known European to sail the St. Lawrence inland from the Atlantic Ocean. He named it in honor of St. Lawrence because he arrived at the river's entrance on that saint's feast day in 1535. The shores of the St. Lawrence were inhabited by the Iroquois—Mohawks to the east, whose reservation today still straddles the river, and Oneidas further inland. To the Indians, the St. Lawrence was a great source of food and an important travel route. To the Europeans, the St. Lawrence was the point of entry for further exploration of the continent's interior.

Still, the navigation problems posed by parts of the river inhibited its use as a major shipping channel, which is why the riverbed was dredged and locks and canals were built. Queen Elizabeth II and President Dwight D. Eisenhower formally opened the newly constructed St. Lawrence Seaway in 1959, and since then large liners and thousands of recreational boaters have routinely traveled between Montreal and Lake Superior. The Erie, Illinois, and New York Barge canal systems provide many points of access from the Mississippi River to the Great Lakes, the Niagara River, and the St. Lawrence Seaway.

State parks, campgrounds, and historic sites abound along the shores of the St. Lawrence, while anglers cast lines for bullhead in the spring and larger fish in the warmer months. Recently, overnight cruises on the St. Lawrence have regained favor with vacationers, too.

"Cartier ascending the St. Lawrence," 1893 lithograph

Rest and relaxation at Bluff Island on the St. Lawrence River, 1900

Postcard view of Thousand Islands region from the air, St. Lawrence Seaway

Thousand Islands region from the air, St. Lawrence Seaway

CASTLES OF THE EMPIRE STATE

Most people associate castles with feudal Europe, enclaves of royalty and overlords. But those who made their fortunes in the New World sometimes had a taste for more than just mansions; their homes were designed as statements of wealth, sophistication, and, in at least one case, boundless love for an adored wife.

Perhaps the most romantic of New York's castles is Boldt Castle, on Heart Island in the St. Lawrence Seaway, not far from Alexandria Bay. Around the turn of the twentieth century, multi-millionaire George C. Boldt, proprietor of the Waldorf-Astoria Hotel in New York City, commissioned the castle as a monument of his love for his wife, Louise. He hired a Philadelphia architect firm to design a replica of a Rhineland castle and spent more than $2.5 million on its construction. Louise died in 1904, and the brokenhearted George ordered all work be stopped. For the next seven decades, the castle and its surrounding buildings were left to the elements, until the Thousand Islands Bridge Authority acquired the island in 1977 and began restoration efforts. Today, visitors tour Boldt Castle by the hundreds between May and October, and the island is a popular site for weddings.

The Hudson River was a prime backdrop for many of New York's early imposing castles, though most disappeared as the Hudson Valley became more heavily populated. Of those that remain, one of the best specimens is Fonthill in The Bronx. Named for Fonthill Abbey, William Beckett's castle in England, Fonthill was built in the mid-1800s as a home for Shakespearean actor Edwin Forrest and his wife. They divorced before ever taking up residence in Fonthill, and the castle was sold to the Sisters of Charity. Today, Fonthill houses administrative and financial aid offices for Mount St. Vincent College.

New York City's other notable castle is in Central Park. Built in 1869, Belvedere Castle sits on Vista Rock, the highest point in the park, overlooking the Great Lawn (which originally was a rectangular reservoir). The U.S. Weather Service took over the New York Meteorological Observatory in 1912 and still collects the park's weather data from the castle today. *Sesame Street* fans will know Belvedere Castle as the home of Count von Count.

Bannerman Castle in the Hudson Highlands was built by Frank Bannerman, a scrap and munitions dealer whose inventory grew so large that he was forced to relocate his business outside New York City limits. He came upon an island in the Hudson River while canoeing, bought it in 1900, and began building an imitation Scottish castle, as well as a modest house, on the site. He and his wife lived there during the summer months. His wife, an avid gardener, landscaped the island with shrubs and flowerbeds, some of which can still be seen today. Visitors are not allowed on the island, but you can travel around it by boat, and the Bannerman Castle Trust Inc. hopes one day to restore the castle and other buildings to a condition that will allow visitors to tour the island on foot.

Opposite: *Belvedere Castle, Central Park, New York City*

Right and below: *Boldt Estate, Heart Island, St. Lawrence River*

"Late Afternoon Calm on the Erie Canal," painting by George Harvey, 1837

ERIE CANAL

As president, Thomas Jefferson understood the strategic value of building a navigable waterway across the wilderness of Upstate New York: It would allow for faster and cheaper movement of people and goods, thus bolstering trade and encouraging Euro-American settlement of the continent's interior, which in turn would offer some protection against French and British encroachment on the United States' claims to the western part of the land.

But building such a waterway also would be expensive and difficult, especially considering the lack of engineering expertise in the newly formed country. "It is a splendid project and may be executed a century hence," Jefferson is reported to have said in 1809 to a New York delegation seeking federal funding for the canal, "but it is a little short of madness to think of it this day."

DeWitt Clinton's campaign for governor touted the canal plan and the prosperity it would bring to the Empire State. He got the state legislature to approve the funding, and from then on, the canal's popularity ebbed and flowed with Clinton's political fortunes. The project was derided as "Clinton's Ditch" or "Clinton's Folly" when he was unpopular, lauded as a tremendous feat of engineering and American ingenuity when he was in good standing.

Eight years and $7 million later, the Erie Canal covered 363 miles from Albany to Buffalo, incorporating eighteen aqueducts and eighty-three locks to accommodate the 500-plus-foot difference in altitude. Travel time and shipping costs plummeted. Westward expansion exploded. By the time it was 100 years old, the Erie Canal had inspired countless imitations and had itself been rebuilt, redirected, and recast as part of the New York State Barge Canal System. After its importance to commerce faded away with the emergence of the railroads, so did the canal itself; many portions of it were filled in to accommodate other kinds of development.

Behind redevelopment efforts that began in the late 1990s, the Erie Canal has come back into its own as a recreational and heritage tourism asset. Towns along the original waterway hold festivals and farmer's markets and countless other events to call attention to their place in history, and recreational boaters, kayakers, hikers, and cyclists are using the canal and towpaths in ever-growing numbers. In 2007, more than 30,000 curious tourists and history buffs turned out to see the *Lois McClure*, a replica of an 1862 Erie Canal schooner, as she traveled from Buffalo to her home in Vermont over the course of 100 days. The same year, a Canadian boat builder made history by taking his solar-powered

Horses pulling packet boat, Erie Canal Village, Rome

pontoon boat—believed to be the first solar vessel to traverse the Erie Canal—on a twelve-day cruise from Oswego.

Although spring floods and dry summers affect the traffic on and along the canal, it remains a viable and vital attraction for many Upstate communities.

Canalfest, Waterford

"A view on the Mohawk River," 1793 etching

Mohawk Valley, east of Little Falls, 1890

THE MOHAWK VALLEY

You could argue that New York City never would have become the international commercial center it is if it weren't for the Mohawk Valley. Stretching about 150 miles from near Albany to Oneida Lake, the Mohawk River was the only navigable east-west water route through the state and the only convenient passage from the east side of the Appalachian Mountains to the fertile Midwest. The Erie Canal paralleled the Mohawk Valley, as did the first railroads to cross the state, opening up a trade line from New York City to the Ohio Valley and beyond.

Although the tribes of the Iroquois Confederacy had established peaceful relations generations earlier and no longer fought over the river's resources, its strategic and economic importance made the Mohawk Valley prime ground for fighting among the European powers that were trying to dominate trade and claim the territory for themselves. Several battles took place here during both the French and Indian War and the American Revolution, the latter depicted in the 1939 John Ford film, *Drums Along the Mohawk*, starring Henry Fonda and Claudette Colbert.

After the Revolutionary War, the villages and cities of the Mohawk Valley became industrial centers. Factories made everything from firearms (Remington Arms in Ilion) to clothing (the knitting mills of Utica and other cities) to silverware (Oneida Ltd. in Oneida) and metalwork (Revere Copper in Rome). The region's economy was so firmly based in manufacturing that when companies began moving south for cheaper labor and lower taxes, many Mohawk Valley communities took decades to recover.

With the increasing popularity of heritage tourism, the Mohawk Valley has begun repositioning itself as a national historic treasure. The Mohawk Valley Heritage Corridor, the first regional heritage area in New York State, connects hundreds of historic and cultural sites, as well as three designated scenic byways, in eight Upstate counties. The Heritage Corridor Commission boasts that visitors today can "still dine in colonial taverns, walk Revolutionary battlefields, explore prehistoric caves and visit canal-era villages."

City of Amsterdam, Mohawk Valley

Opposite: *Mohawk Valley, with Interstate 90*

Mills at Little Falls, Herkimer County, 1941

Harmony Mill, Cohoes, Albany County

MANUFACTURING AND SMALL INDUSTRY

The Erie Canal and the Industrial Revolution were kind to New York. The former allowed for cheap shipping of raw materials and finished goods from small Upstate villages to markets far and wide, and the latter made more of those finished goods affordable to more people. From garment factories in New York City to furniture, glass, and gunmakers Upstate, virtually every region of New York depended in some measure on manufacturing. Even the tiny community of Cleveland, on the north shore of Oneida Lake, was once home to three glass factories.

In the village of Ilion in Herkimer County, a son of a blacksmith, dissatisfied with the quality of rifles he was able to purchase, established his own firearm business, Remington Arms. Since 1816, the company has gone through many incarnations and owners, but it is the oldest company in the nation that still makes its original product.

Towns located along the Erie Canal and later the railroads, such as Little Falls, Utica, and Rome, were ideal locations for manufacturers. Rochester is still home to Eastman Kodak, which expanded from film and cameras to photocopiers, medical imaging, chemicals (since spun off into a separate company), and batteries. Although many of its manufacturing operations have moved to other locations, the corporate headquarters is still located in downtown Rochester, and research and some manufacturing are still carried out in Kodak Park.

Traditional manufacturing in New York took a series of body blows in the 1970s as rising taxes, labor costs, and utility rates sent many factories south or overseas. It took some time, but gradually high-tech start-ups and established companies began filling the void traditional manufacturing had left. Advanced Micro Devices Inc. is planning to build a $3.2 billion computer chip fabrication plant in Saratoga in 2009, building on the emerging nanotechnology industry already in the area. In Rome, the former Griffiss Air Force Base is now a technology park, populated by a variety of small manufacturing concerns, many of them in medical services. And in New Hartford, a suburb of Utica, a manufacturer of plastic forms bought the molds and the rights to the once-ubiquitous plastic pink flamingo, and the company began making the Americana icons in 2007.

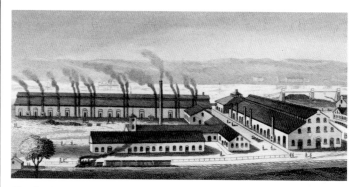

Burden Iron Works, Troy, 1876

Utica panorama, 1909

UTICA

Perhaps no Upstate city was hit as hard by the decline of manufacturing in the Northeast as Utica. Long a center for knitting mills and tool and die factories, and at one point known as "the radio capital of the world," thanks to a General Electric plant that employed as many as 8,000 people, by the 1990s residents were sporting bumper stickers that read, "Last One Out of Utica, Please Turn Out the Lights." Its reputation for political corruption and general vice from the 1930s to the 1950s earned it the moniker "Sin City," and its decline as part of the Northeastern Rust Belt led many to call it "the city that God forgot."

It wasn't always that way. Though Utica was plundered and burned by British forces during the Revolutionary War, it prospered with the construction of the Erie Canal. The first section of the canal linked Rome and Syracuse, and the later Chenango Canal connected Utica and Binghamton, opening markets for Utica business and industry in the Southern Tier and northern Pennsylvania. Utica's knitting mills employed thousands and are credited with inventing the "union suit," the long underwear, usually red, with a button flap on the rear.

Though recovery has been slow following the economic stagnation that began after World War II, Utica does show signs of picking itself up. Its arts community is greatly enhanced by the presence of the Munson-Williams-Proctor Institute, dubbed "the Munstitute" by locals, which combines an excellent art gallery with classes in various art forms. The Stanley Theater for the Performing Arts in Utica's downtown is a showcase for concerts and stage productions, and there are several thriving venues for jazz and other music genres. It's also home to the annual Boilermaker Road Race, the largest 15-kilometer run in the United States, attracting runners from all over the world, and Central New York's largest winter festival, Snowfari, where winter sports enthusiasts can qualify for the Winter Empire State Games.

Not all manufacturing has left Utica. The Matt Brewing Company, makers of Saranac and other beer brands, is the oldest continuously operating brewery in New York. It's now under the leadership of the family's third and fourth generations, and visitors can tour the brewery year-round.

Downtown Utica, including the "Gold Dome" Bank and State Office Building

ROME AND FORT STANWIX

The Oneida Indians called the site of present-day Rome "the Great Carrying Place." The nearly two-mile portage between the Mohawk River and Wood Creek had to be traversed to continue the journey to the Great Lakes. In the early 1800s, the Erie Canal was begun at the Great Carrying Place, and its construction turned Rome into a building and commercial center virtually overnight. With the Industrial Revolution, Rome's metal production facilities earned it the nickname "The Copper City"; during its heyday, Rome produced about 10 percent of all U.S. copper.

In the 1950s, Griffiss Air Force Base supported Rome's economy with about 5,000 military and civilian jobs. The base was closed in 1995, but two key aspects of the operation remain today: Rome Lab, now called the Rome Research Site, which has developed several cutting-edge technologies for the Air Force; and the Northeast Air Defense Sector. Over the past decade, Griffiss has been redeveloped as a business and industrial park, and the city's high school was relocated to a new, larger building there. Developers also are in the process of converting former base housing into a resort-style planned community. The city celebrates its patriot and canal-era heritage with an annual "Honor America Days" festival that attracts thousands of visitors.

In the 1750s, the British built Fort Stanwix near the Great Carrying Place to protect this critical juncture in the fur trade. The fort was abandoned after the French and Indian War, and American colonists rebuilt it during the Revolutionary War.

In January 1777, British General John Burgoyne was inspired with what he considered a brilliant plan to quash the troublesome American rebellion once and for all. A three-pronged attack from the north, west, and south, he reasoned, would virtually eliminate the military threat in New York and cut off New England—the heart of the rebellion—from the rest of the colonies.

That summer, Burgoyne's forces traveled from Montreal down Lake Champlain and the Hudson to Albany, capturing Fort Ticonderoga on the way. At Albany, Burgoyne was to meet up with General Barry St. Leger, who was heading east from the British stronghold at Oswego. General William Howe, in charge in British-occupied New York City, was to come up the Hudson.

But Howe, worried that rebel forces would recapture New York City, decided to attack George Washington's troops in

Fort Stanwix, eighteenth-century drawing

Philadelphia instead. Meanwhile, St. Leger had problems of his own: The fort at the Great Carrying Place was far better protected than he expected. When his demand for surrender was met with sneering defiance by young fort commander Peter Gansevoort, St. Leger's troops settled down for a siege on August 3, 1777.

General Nicholas Herkimer directing his troops at the Battle of Oriskany, August 6, 1777

Re-enactors at Fort Stanwix National Monument

Forty miles away, General Nicholas Herkimer gathered some 800 militia men, accompanied by at least sixty Oneidas, to come to the fort's rescue. On August 6, Herkimer's troops were ambushed by British troops and their Iroquois (mainly Mohawk) allies near the village of Oriskany. The air became thick with the smoke from musket fire and the screams of the wounded and dying. Herkimer, his horse killed and his leg shattered from a musket ball, famously directed his troops from the shelter of a beech tree. Han Yerry, an Oneida man whose wife and son also fought in the battle, was wounded in the wrist but kept fighting; his wife, Two Kettles, loaded his gun for him.

The six-hour battle claimed all but about 150 of Herkimer's militia, making it one of the bloodiest battles in U.S. history. St. Leger's failure to capture Fort Stanwix after a twenty-one-day siege and the ferocity of the battle at Oriskany demoralized the British and ultimately led to Burgoyne's surrender at Saratoga, which in turn convinced the French to support the colonists in their bid for independence.

Today, Oriskany Battlefield is a state historic site, with an obelisk erected in 1877 to mark the one-hundredth anniversary of the battle. A commemoration ceremony on August 6 each year celebrates the heroism and sacrifice of both patriots and loyalists who gave their lives to defend their beliefs. The original Fort Stanwix is long gone, but in the 1970s, the city of Rome built a re-creation, which is now part of the National Park Service. At Fort Stanwix National Monument, re-enactors demonstrate eighteenth-century life for visitors, reflecting the eclectic mix of American, English, Dutch, and Indian residents and traders at the fort.

Reconstructed Fort Stanwix National Monument, Rome

Aerial view of Doubleday Field and the village of Cooperstown, 1954

COOPERSTOWN

Cooperstown is best known as the home of the National Baseball Hall of Fame, and legend says that Abner Doubleday invented the national pastime on a pasture in the village in 1839. Although the Doubleday myth has been debunked by baseball scholars, locals and most baseball fans don't really care. The Hall of Fame brings the current stars of the sport here every July for Induction Day and keeps the memory of baseball's glory days alive every other day of the year. The business district of Cooperstown has capitalized on the popularity of the Hall of Fame, and storefronts that used to house grocery and hardware stores now are filled with memorabilia shops and other services catering largely to the tourists who flock to the region every summer.

There's more to Cooperstown than baseball, though. The New York State Historical Association's library is located here, as are the Farmer's Museum and the Fenimore Art Museum. The Clark family, whose fortune was built on a half-share in the Singer Sewing Machine patent, has left its mark throughout the area, too, with dozens of donations for community projects such as

Main Street during Hall of Fame induction weekend, 2005

Lippitt Barnyard, Farmer's Museum

parks and education scholarships, as well as the land for the local high school. The Clark family's holdings in the village include the lush Otesaga Inn, the Cooper Inn, and founding and continuing interests in both the Baseball Hall of Fame and the Mary Imogene Bassett Hospital.

The village was founded after the Revolutionary War by William Cooper, a judge and member of Congress who encouraged others to settle here, on the southern tip of Otsego Lake. Cooper's mansion burned down some years ago, but many of the stone houses he built still exist, and these help give the village its old-world atmosphere still today. The grounds of Cooper's former estate are now in use as a park.

William's son was the famous novelist James Fenimore Cooper, author of *The Last of the Mohicans*. James dubbed this region of New York "Leatherstocking Country," and he called the lake "Glimmerglass," a term that was later adopted by the Glimmerglass Opera.

Since 1975, Glimmerglass Opera near Cooperstown has presented its summer season of new and lesser-known operas in a repertory format. Often working in conjunction with the New York City Opera, Glimmerglass has hosted the American or world premieres of several works. Young adult singers just beginning their professional careers also come to Glimmerglass to study and perform through the Young American Artists program. They give solo recitals in the Cooperstown area and learn both performing techniques and behind-the-scenes skills, such as preparing for auditions and managing the business side of their careers.

Glimmerglass Opera's first season consisted of four performances of *La Bohème* in the Cooperstown High School Auditorium. Since 1987, the institution has operated from its own quarters, the Alice Busch Opera Theater, located on forty-three acres of donated land about eight miles north of Cooperstown. A typical summer season at Glimmerglass consists of four works and a total of about forty performances.

First incarnation of the Polo Grounds, 1887 lithograph

BASEBALL IN NEW YORK

The enduring legend that Abner Doubleday invented the game in a pasture in Cooperstown in 1839 notwithstanding, modern baseball—an amalgamation of various ages-old games from Europe—can trace its roots to New York City in 1845. That's when Alexander J. Cartwright organized the New York Knickerbocker Base Ball Club and wrote down the rules for the game. Whether he invented those rules on his own or merely collected and organized them isn't known, but even today his writings are referred to as the "Original Rules of Baseball."

New York State has a number of minor league baseball teams, but fans have always looked to New York City for The Show. From the Polo Grounds and Ebbets Field (which were demolished by the same wrecking ball in the 1960s) to the new Yankee Stadium and the Mets' Citi Field—both set to open for the 2009 season—many of baseball's richest and most memorable moments have occurred in New York City. New York's Major League teams (the Yankees, Giants, Mets, and Dodgers) have won thirty-four World Series titles, twenty-six of them by the Yankees.

In addition, minor league and semipro teams at all levels provide excitement and entertainment for many communities around the state. Buffalo is home to the Bisons of the Triple-A International League, and the Chiefs, also in the International League, play in Syracuse. At the Single-A level, the New York–Penn League has teams in Auburn (the Doubledays), Batavia (the Muckdogs), Jamestown (the Jammers), Oneonta (the Tigers), Troy (the Tri-City ValleyCats), Wappingers Falls (the Hudson Valley Renegades), and the boroughs of Brooklyn (the Cyclones) and Staten Island (the Yankees).

New Yankee Stadium under construction next to old Yankee Stadium, 2008

Tri-City ValleyCats game at Joseph L. Bruno Stadium, Troy

Left: *Brooklyn Cyclones vs. Staten Island Yankees, Keyspan Park, Coney Island*

FOOTBALL IN NEW YORK

New York Giants football game at the Polo Grounds, circa 1930s

Ironically, neither of the two National Football League teams with "New York" in their names actually plays in New York. Both the Giants and the Jets moved across the river to East Rutherford, New Jersey, the Giants in 1976 and the Jets in 1984. The defection so angered Ed Koch, then mayor of New York City, that he refused to honor the Giants when they won the Super Bowl in 1987.

In fact, until the Giants' upset victory over the previously undefeated New England Patriots in Super Bowl XLII on February 3, 2008, New York City had never given a tickertape parade in honor of a football team. It was one extra dash of history to crown the Giants' championship.

All three of New York's pro football teams have some claim to fame. The Buffalo Bills remain the only NFL team to play in four consecutive Super Bowls. They also hold the ignominious record of losing four in a row: to the Giants in 1991, to Washington in 1992, and to Dallas in 1993 and 1994.

The Jets set the precedent for the Giants' 2008 upset back in 1969 by beating Baltimore in Super Bowl III. Quarterback Joe Namath proved not only that his team could defeat the heavily favored Colts, but that the American Football League, of which the Jets were members, could compete with the National Football League. The Jets joined the NFL the following year.

New York Giants players celebrate a touchdown during Super Bowl XLII

BASKETBALL IN NEW YORK

A.A.A.U. Champion New York University basketball team, 1920

New York Knicks players Harry Gallatin (11) and Nate "Sweetwater" Clifton (8), circa 1950s

New York Knick Jamal Crawford, against the Miami Heat, 2008

New York has a prominent place in the history of basketball. The New York Knickerbockers (more commonly known as the Knicks now) played the Toronto Huskies in 1946 in what the National Basketball Association deems the first game of the league's history. In fact, the Knicks were then part of the Basketball Association of America, the first concerted effort by team owners to play the game in major cities. Out of the league's original eight teams, only the Knicks and Boston Celtics remain in their original cities.

Another of those original teams, the Syracuse Nationals, moved to Philadelphia in the 1960s and became the 76ers, but not before Nationals owner Danny Biasone convinced the league to institute a 24-second shot clock to add more action to the game. Biasone had noticed that fans got bored watching the common stalling tactics of teams who were leading; before the shot clock, players could simply pass the ball around endlessly and never attempt a shot. The shot clock served to increase the average score of a game by more than ten points; many historians say it saved the game. A monument to the shot clock stands in Syracuse's Armory Square.

College basketball is popular in New York, too. Marist and St. John's both play Division I basketball, as does Syracuse University, whose men's team won the NCAA Championship in 2003. City College of New York won the championship in 1950, although the school no longer participates in Division I athletics.

One of the most famous basketball teams ever, the Harlem Globetrotters, was actually formed in Chicago in the 1920s. The exhibition team took the name of the New York City neighborhood because of its strong connections to African American life and culture.

SYRACUSE

Some say Syracuse was the city that salt built. Its marshy swamps were extremely salty, and you didn't have to dig or mine it; you could just boil the water until only the salt remained. Before refrigeration, salt was a critical ingredient in preserving food.

Before the late 1700s, the area was the territory of the Onondaga Indians and the center of the centuries-old Iroquois Confederacy. According to Iroquois legend, the Peacemaker who brought the previously warring nations together uprooted a tree on the shores of Onondaga Lake (now the site of the Carousel Center mall) and cast the weapons of war into the pit—a legend that is credited as the origin of the phrase "bury the hatchet." French missionaries came here in the 1600s, but the area wasn't heavily settled until after the Revolutionary War, when a nearly bankrupt federal government awarded tracts of land as payment to patriot soldiers.

Syracuse, named for a Sicilian village that early residents thought was similar to this area, really gained prominence when the Erie Canal reached Onondaga Lake. The arrival of the canal made the city an important trading and manufacturing center. Demand for salt started the building boom, but even after refrigeration became commonplace and salt manufacturing declined, the city was home to several other industries. Gustav Stickley, a leading spokesman for the Arts and Crafts Movement that deplored the shoddy quality of Industrial Revolution–era goods, and his brothers made their distinctive furniture here. Syracuse China, with its distinctive white glaze, won a Medal of Honor at the 1893 World Fair. The serrated knife; the Brannock Device, which is used to measure feet for shoes; and the air-cooled automobile engine were all invented in Syracuse. Crouse Hinds, now a part of Cooper Industries, began here making electric car headlights. The founders also are credited with inventing the traffic light, the first of which was installed at the intersection of James and State Streets in 1924.

In the years leading up to the Civil War, Syracuse was known as the "great central depot on the Underground Railroad." Prominent abolitionists included Gerrit Smith and members of the Unitarian Church in Syracuse and the Quakers in nearby Skaneateles. In 1851, several hundred people broke into the city jail to free a former slave known as Jerry, who had been arrested under the Fugitive Slave Act; the "Jerry Rescue" is still commemorated today.

Like many Rust Belt cities, Syracuse lost businesses, jobs, and population beginning in the 1970s, and it has struggled to rebuild its economy. The presence of Syracuse University, LeMoyne College, and Onondaga Community College have helped the city recast itself as a major center for medical services and teaching, information technology, and other fields. Its collection of parks—notably Burnet Park, which boasts the nation's first public golf course and a nationally respected zoo—and cultural activities, including the annual Jazz Fest and Sammy Awards for local and regional musicians, along with revitalization of areas like Armory Square into mixed-use neighborhoods, also have helped attract young people back to the city.

Syracuse Savings Bank, North Salina Street, circa 1900

Erie Canal at Salina Street, 1904

Below: *Clinton Square, on the former site of the Erie Canal*

Postcard view of state fair grounds and buildings, Syracuse

Postcard view of state fair grounds

GREAT NEW YORK STATE FAIR

Outsiders and even Downstaters might think of New York as a financial or fashion center, but the Empire State was founded as a farming colony, and agriculture remains among its top industries today. The annual celebration of New York's agricultural roots, the twelve-day Great New York State Fair, features thousands of competitors in livestock, horticulture, baking, crafts, and countless other categories. Exhibits showcasing the history of rural New York life include demonstrations of broom- and soap-making, woodworking, cooking over an open fire, and weaving. There are also collections of antique carriages and early automobiles, historic trains, and an Iroquois Indian village that offers both contemporary and historic exhibits of the Six Nations Confederacy.

The fair got its start in 1841, when the state legislature appropriated $8,000 for the "promotion of agriculture and household manufacturers in the State" through an annual fair. It was the first event of its kind in the still-young United States. Syracuse, not yet graced with a city charter, was selected as the site for the fair because it was the midway point on the Erie Canal and a significant station for the rapidly developing rail lines between Albany and Buffalo. Between 10,000 and 15,000 people turned out for the two-day event, despite heavy rains that turned the grounds into a muddy mess.

For the next few decades, the fair traveled among the larger Upstate villages and cities, finally coming to rest permanently in Syracuse in 1890. Since the beginning, fairgoers have been attracted by the varied bounty of New York's fields and orchards, demonstrations of farming and household techniques new and old, and, of course, the midway rides. According to *The Empire Showcase: A History of the New York State Fair*, in 1849, forty-four years before the Ferris Wheel was introduced at the 1893 Columbian Exposition, the New York State Fair midway boasted a very similar ride. The device was built of iron and wood and stood fifty feet high; large buckets positioned at each of the wheel's compass points could hold four adults or six children, and the wheel turned via a system of ropes, carrying the passengers aloft, affording them spectacular views of the fairgrounds, Syracuse, and the gently rolling Central New York countryside.

Auto and motorcycle racing have been favorite features of the fair since the early twentieth century, and today large crowds turn out both for the fair's annual stock car races and for a variety of auto shows, including the famous Syracuse Nationals show. Between 900,000 and 1 million people visit the Great New York State Fair every year, and the grounds attract another 1 million visitors the rest of the year for boat shows, RV shows, the annual Home & Garden Show, and a full schedule of other exhibitions, concerts, conventions, and educational events.

Great New York State Fair, Syracuse, 2005

Draft-horse competition, Great New York State Fair, 2005

Amish farm near Martinsburg, Lewis County

Roadside farm stand in Naples, Ontario County

FARMING AND AGRICULTURE

For centuries before the Dutch and other European settlers arrived in what is now New York State, the natives had been cultivating crops in the region's arable valleys and flat lands. They practiced companion planting; instead of dedicating acres to a single crop, they planted corn, beans, and squash—the Three Sisters, sustainers of life, in Native American tradition—together in a process that modern agriculturalists call "the genius of the Indians." The corn provided support for the beans and shade for the squash; the beans provided nitrogen to nourish the soil; and the squash trapped moisture. Some Native Americans still practice this method of farming on a small scale. The Oneida Indian Nation near Syracuse, for example, devotes about fifty acres of its agricultural operations to a "Nation garden," where it grows traditional white corn, beans, squash, and ceremonial tobacco for its members.

Although the Dutch were drawn to present-day New York State by the excellent fur trade, they soon expanded into farming. Greenwich Village and even parts of Central Park were farmland

for generations, and as settlements expanded westward, farming was the cornerstone of the economy. Even today, when many family farms have been absorbed by huge corporate concerns or annexed by villages and cities for development, agriculture accounts for $3.6 billion a year in New York's economy.

And the products of the state are diverse. New York is the country's third-leading milk producer and the second-largest apple producer. Cabbage, onions, sweet corn, tart cherries, strawberries, pears, snap peas, pumpkins, cucumbers, squash, and cauliflower—all are leading agricultural products for New York.

Perhaps the best feature of New York's agricultural industry is the plethora of farmer's markets and fruit and vegetable stands that dot the roadways statewide during the warmer months. Particularly Upstate, New Yorkers know winter is really over when the roadside stands shed their winter shutters and begin hanging baskets of flowers and putting out tables of freshly picked fruits and vegetables.

Farm and home in Cayuga County, 1875 lithograph

Below: *Dairy farm in Copake, Columbia County*

"Johnny Appleseed" showing settlers how to plant apple trees, nineteenth-century drawing

ORCHARDS AND VINEYARDS

Apples and grapes have been important segments of New York's agricultural economy almost since the New Amsterdam colony was founded. Dutch governor Peter Stuyvesant planted an apple tree from Holland at the corner of Third Avenue and 13th Street in Manhattan in 1647, and it didn't take long for orchards to pop up all over Long Island and the Hudson Valley. By the 1700s, Native Americans and European settlers alike were planting and tending apple orchards. The settlers used the apples to make cider, vinegar, and hard cider, and "apple bees" were common fall affairs. In the late 1700s, John Chapman, better known as Johnny Appleseed, planted his first orchard at his uncle's farm in Olean before moving on to Pennsylvania, Ohio, and points west.

Many of the apples you find in your local grocery store originated in New York; more than 500 varieties were developed here by the 1850s, including the New Pippin, Northern Spy, Jonathan, and McIntosh. Today, New York is the second-largest apple producer in the United States, with orchards based mainly

Hudson River vineyard, 1867 engraving

along the southern shore of Lake Ontario and in the Hudson and upper Lake Champlain valleys.

Winemaking also has a long history in New York, though it's a bit younger than the apple-growing industry. The first winery

Bully Hill Vineyards, Finger Lakes region

Below: *Harvest time at apple orchard, Montgomery County*

in the state was Brotherhood Winery, established in the Hudson Valley in 1839 and now the oldest continuously operating winery in the United States. Between the 1860s and the 1880s, several wineries opened in the Finger Lakes. Farm wineries—small operations that generally produced only a few thousand gallons a year—began springing up in the 1960s and '70s, and proliferated enormously after 1976, when the Farm Winery Act made these smaller operations more economically viable. Of the more than 200 wineries in New York State today, less than two dozen were established before 1976. There are wineries in virtually every sector of the state, but most are concentrated in four areas: Long Island, the Hudson Valley, the southern shore of Lake Erie, and the Finger Lakes.

New York ranks third in the nation in production of wine and juice grapes, behind California and Washington. The state's grape crop is worth some $30 million a year, but the real money in New York's wineries comes from tourism: More than three million people a year visit the state's wineries, taking tours of the smaller operations and often spending several days in one of the winemaking regions to explore other attractions.

FINGER LAKES

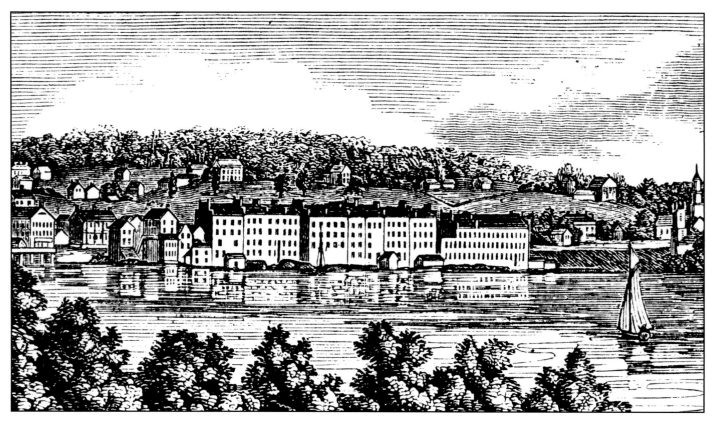

Wood engraving of Skaneateles waterfront, 1841

According to Native American legend, the Finger Lakes were formed when the Great Spirit laid his hand down on the land and left an impression of his five fingers in the earth. More likely the result of glacial shifts during the last Ice Age, these long, narrow, and deep lakes have been natural sites for human habitation for centuries. The region was long a part of Iroquois territory, and two of the lakes are named for Iroquois member tribes, Cayuga and Seneca. Other tribes who fled European encroachment in the Carolinas and other southern regions also settled around the Finger Lakes, having sought the friendship and protection of the Iroquois. Ganondagan State Historic Site, the only one in the state system dedicated to the history of New York's original inhabitants, focuses on the history and culture of the Seneca and has as its centerpiece a replica of a bark-covered longhouse, the traditional dwelling of the Iroquois.

The topography and climate of the Finger Lakes makes it ideal wine country, because the grapes are sheltered from early

Skaneateles waterfront

View of Lake Keuka and vineyards

frost in the spring and right before harvest. There are more than 100 wineries in the region, making it New York's largest wine-producing area and second-largest in the nation, behind only California's Napa Valley. The wineries also anchor the region's tourism industry; visitors spend some $200 million a year, and the tourism and hospitality sector employs about 15,000 people.

The Finger Lakes also is dairy farm country, with many of the farms run by Amish or Mennonite families who have been on the land for generations. Farms also produce corn, wheat, barley, and soybeans, as well as cabbage, sweet corn, potatoes, honey, and maple syrup.

Fishing and recreational boating are popular pastimes, and many visitors are attracted to the natural beauty of the Finger Lakes. These remnants of the last Ice Age feature unique glens and falls, created by the erosion of the shale and other sedimentary rock, and many state parks and recreation areas have been built around the gorges and other natural features here.

Postcard view of Lake Keuka, near Penn Yann

Elizabeth Cady Stanton addressing the first Women's Rights Convention in Seneca Falls, 1848

SENECA FALLS

Seneca Falls doesn't actually have falls anymore. The series of small falls and rapids were engineered out of the Seneca River for ease of navigation in 1818 and later as part of the Erie Canal. But this village owes its existence to those falls, which provided water power for several operations, including tanneries, distilleries, and mills. A short distance upstream, a small hydroelectric generating station still operates today.

The village gained fame for its role in the women's suffrage movement of the mid-nineteenth century. The first Women's Rights Convention was held here in 1848, and Amelia Bloomer lent her name to a new form of ladies' undergarments when she popularized them in her newspaper, *The Lily*. Today, the village is home to the Women's Rights National Historical Park and the National Women's Hall of Fame, which recognizes women for their leadership, courage, and contributions to society. Altogether, the Hall of Fame has inducted 226 women; Senator Hillary Clinton, the first female senator from New York, was inducted in 2005. Ironically, Seneca Falls didn't get its first female village administrator until 1998, and its first female mayor wasn't elected until 2004.

"When Anthony Met Stanton" statue on Seneca Falls canal promenade

Fall Street, Seneca Falls

WATKINS GLEN

Since shortly after World War II, Watkins Glen has been known mainly for its place in auto racing history. But even people who have never heard of NASCAR or the Watkins Glen International Speedway are drawn to this village for the spectacular Watkins Glen Gorge. The first formal trail through the gorge was built by a private individual in the 1860s, and it became so popular that the state purchased the gorge and surrounding land in 1906 and made it a state park, the first in the Finger Lakes region. During the Great Depression, members of the Civilian Conservation Corps built stone paths and pavilions through the park to replace the weaker (and higher maintenance) wood plank walkways. By the 1980s, the gorge attracted a million visitors a year.

Originally an Iroquois stronghold, the area around Watkins Glen was devastated by Major-General John Sullivan's campaign to punish and drive out the Iroquois who had sided with the British during the Revolutionary War. In the mid-1800s, European settlers moved into the area, and the natural springs (and their supposed healing powers) naturally led to the development of a spa. In *The Mineral Waters of the United States and Their Therapeutic Uses*, published in 1899, author James K. Crook, A.M., M.D., compared the spring waters at Watkins Glen to "those of Kissingen, Homburg, and Wiesbaden." Some waters were used strictly for bathing or to treat gout, rheumatic diseases, sciatica, and lumbago; others were prescribed for drinking to aid with digestion and even treat issues such as anemia and "chronic renal diseases."

In 1948, the village held the first post–World War II road race in the country, the Watkins Glen Sports Car Grand Prix. The course ran through the village; a checkered flag decorates the original start/finish line on the village's main street. A permanent racing facility was built in the 1950s, and it has hosted nearly every type of auto race, including Formula One and, of course, the annual NASCAR race—one of only two road-course races in NASCAR's season.

Rainbow Falls, Watkins Glen State Park

Postcard view of Rainbow Falls, Watkins Glen State Park

View of Cornell University and Ithaca from McGraw Tower, 1902

ITHACA

The small city of Ithaca had big dreams of becoming a major commercial center when the canal and railway systems made their appearance, but its destiny lay in a different direction, and most of today's residents wouldn't trade their Ithaca for anything the city's founders envisioned. In the eighteenth century, Ithaca was infamous for gambling, horse racing, liquor, swearing, and breaking the Sabbath, earning it the label of "Sodom" before the name was officially changed to Ithaca. Most of the references to the city's early reputation have long since faded away, with the notable exception of Lucifer Falls at Robert H. Treman State Park.

Ezra Cornell founded Cornell University here in 1865. The institution was unusual in two respects: It was open to women, and it wasn't affiliated with any religious organization. With its 20,000 students, Cornell supports much of the city's economy, as do high-tech industry and tourism. Many people from surrounding counties commute to work in Ithaca, and the city has been largely buffered

McGraw Tower, Cornell University

from the economic doldrums much of Upstate has experienced in recent decades. In 2006, it was one of the few Upstate communities that could boast of both economic and population growth.

As befits a liberal college town, Ithaca is home to a number of small businesses that cater to niche markets: vegetarian restaurants, used bookstores, craft stores, and theaters that specialize in "art" and independent films. One of its most famous fixtures is the Moosewood Restaurant, a vegetarian restaurant run as a cooperative. Nearly a dozen Moosewood cookbooks have been published, and *Bon Appétit* magazine named it one of the most influential restaurants of the twentieth century.

Postcard advertising Ithaca's waterfalls and gorges

Downtown Commons, Ithaca

State Street, Ithaca, circa 1890s

CORNING

ention the city of Corning, and most people immediately think of Corning Glass Works. The Fortune 500 company, now known as Corning Inc., still has its headquarters here, and the Corning Museum of Glass is famous both for its collection of glass from throughout history and for its educational programs, particularly one in which children draw designs and glassmakers turn their designs into reality. The city also is known for the Rockwell Museum of Western Art, which has earned Corning rankings among the top small arts towns in the United States.

Corning's first industry, begun after the Revolutionary War, was timber. The Chemung River and, later, feeder canals that connected to New York's main canal system, facilitated the movement of lumber from Corning to other markets, and at one time the great lumber mills of Corning were considered the biggest in the world. But as forests were cleared and timber companies had to move farther afield to harvest their wood, the timber traffic on the river slowed down, and eventually the mills moved north to still-forested areas.

Near the city of Corning is Painted Post, so named because European settlers found a carved wood post bearing the images of twenty-eight men, all painted red, near the confluence of the Cohocton, Tioga, and Canisteo Rivers. No one knows who carved the post or why it was erected at that spot, but when a permanent settlement was established there, the settlers adopted the name Painted Post. Today, the community preserves its past at the historic Benjamin Patterson Inn, a one-room schoolhouse, and other sites from the nineteenth century.

Erie Railway station, circa 1900s

Display, Corning Museum of Glass

Glass blower, Corning Museum of Glass

Rockwell Museum of Western Art

Religion in New York

Unlike colonies in New England, which were founded principally as religious enclaves and had very little tolerance for nonconforming beliefs, the Empire State was founded as a commercial venture, and there was no religious test to join the activities at New Amsterdam. The Dutch were so eager for new settlers that they actively recruited people from all backgrounds.

This isn't to say religious freedom was a given. That principle wasn't established in the New World until the mid-1600s, when a group of farmers in what is now Flushing, Queens, wrote and signed the Flushing Remonstrance. Known as the Magna Carta for religious freedom, the document petitioned for "freedom of conscience" in New Amsterdam in defense of Quakers. Peter Stuyvesant, the director general of the colony, had the farmers arrested, but eventually he was overruled by the Dutch West India Company, and religious tolerance became the law of the colony. This principle carried over into English rule and was famously made into one of the founding tenets of the United States.

In the mid-1770s, an offshoot of a British Protestant sect came to New York City and soon established a communal settlement north of Albany. The Shakers—so named for their ritual trembling and fidgety dance movement—established other communities in New York and New England, including the New Lebanon Society in Columbia County. The Shakers were a celibate society that believed strongly in the segregation of the sexes. They filled their ranks through adoption and conversion, and membership dwindled in the latter half of the nineteenth century. The Shaker legacy lives on today through their quality furniture and craftsmanship, as well as songs and hymnals. The Shaker Museum and Library in Old Chatham and the Mount Lebanon Shaker Village in New Lebanon preserve and celebrate Shaker history and culture.

In the 1820s, Joseph Smith had a vision of an angel, who led him to the location of sacred texts near Palmyra, a few miles east of Rochester. He translated the plates and published the manuscript as *The Book of Mormon*; within a week of publication, Rochester newspapers denounced Smith's work as blasphemy. Undeterred, Smith established The Church of Jesus Christ of Latter-Day Saints in a log cabin in Fayette and baptized his congregation in Seneca Lake. Persecution led Smith to move his church westward; in

"Circular Dance of Shakers," 1872 engraving

1844, he was killed by a mob in Illinois, but the church survived.

Four years after Smith's death, Vermont native John Humphrey Noyes founded the Oneida Community in what is now the city of Sherrill. Based on the communal teachings of first-century Christians, the entire group worked, learned, and made business decisions together; men and women were encouraged to engage in frequent lovemaking with any partner they chose; and reason, music, and art were celebrated as much as spirituality. The Oneida Community enjoyed its version of Eden for thirty-three years; then, when the commune broke up, the group formed Oneida Ltd., the famous silverware maker, to distribute the commune's assets to members. Today, visitors can stay in the Mansion House, which also is home to some fifty permanent residents, and browse through the nineteenth-century library and museum dedicated to the Oneida Community's history.

Stone barn, Mount Lebanon Shaker Village, Columbia County

Temple of Church of Latter-Day Saints, Palmyra

Genesee River and Rochester skyline, 1914

ROCHESTER

The Erie Canal turned Rochester into the "Flour City" and one of the nation's first bona fide boom towns. The first U.S. Census, in 1820, counted only about 1,500 non–Native American residents; within two years of the canal's completion, Rochester was home to ten flour mills, nine sawmills, eight hotels, and 160 canal boats. By the time the settlement was incorporated as a city in 1834, the population had exploded to more than 13,000, and by the time of the Civil War, Rochester boasted a larger population than Chicago, Detroit, or Cleveland.

The "Flour City" moniker came from the city's extensive flour mills, which sprouted up virtually overnight as the Erie Canal made shipping cheaper and easier than ever before. In 1834, the city's twenty mills produced a half million barrels of flour, and within eight years it claimed the title of flour-producing capital of the world. But westward expansion and the settlement of even more fertile land in the Ohio Valley made Rochester's prominence in the manufacture of flour short-lived. It reinvented itself in the late 1850s as the "Flower City," thanks in large part to an entrepreneurial nursery owner named James Vick, who began expanding his business by selling garden seeds through the mail.

Rochester also is the birthplace of a number of inventions and well-known corporations, including Bausch & Lomb, Kodak-Eastman, and Xerox. Western Union was born here in the 1850s and became the driving force for coast-to-coast telegraphic communications. Rochester's Jesse Hatch invented a machine to sew shoe soles and uppers together; Jacob H. Meyer invented the voting machine in the 1890s. In 1931, as the country slid further into the Great Depression, fourteen Rochester-area employers came up with the country's first organized unemployment insurance program.

Today's Rochester earns high marks for its business climate, recreational and cultural offerings, and general livability. It ranks among the top 20 percent of U.S. metro areas for business opportunities and among the top five "creative centers" for innovation. Its relatively low cost of living, unemployment,

Upper Falls of the Genesee River at Rochester, 1836 lithograph

Powers Building, 1904

Powers Building

commute times, and crime rates make it one of the least stressful cities in the country, and *Men's Health* magazine ranked Rochester the third-healthiest city in the nation for men.

The University of Rochester and Rochester Institute of Technology attract young people from all over the globe. World-renowned golf courses, the Rochester Philharmonic Orchestra, 12,000 acres of parkland in surrounding Monroe County, no less than seven sports teams, and annual events such as the High Falls Film Festival and the Rochester International Jazz Festival add to the city's attractiveness for residents and visitors alike.

Upper Falls of the Genesee River and Rochester skyline

John Philip Sousa at Chautauqua Institution, 1925

CHAUTAUQUA LAKE

I n the seventeenth and eighteenth centuries, Chautauqua Lake was part of the water route between Canada and Louisiana, facilitating exploration of the North American continent. But by the early 1800s, it was a summer haven for wealthy tourists, and development around the lake catered mainly to those visitors, who soon began building cabins for extended stays on the shore. The first hotel, opened in 1836, was called the Temperance House; as demand for lodging grew, more hotels sprouted.

The Chautauqua Institution was born here in 1874 as the Chautauqua Lake Sunday School Assembly, founded by two Methodists as an experiment in vacation learning for Sunday school teachers. It was so successful that it almost immediately broadened its curriculum to include topics with more mass appeal, including music, art, physical education, and traditional academic subjects.

Today, the Chautauqua Institution welcomes some 140,000 visitors a year to its public events, and about 7,500 people attend each of its nine-week resident sessions. The institution's Chautauqua Summer Schools offer courses for more than 8,000 students in the performing arts, writing, and other special interests.

Chautauqua Lake, 1908

Boat dock, Chautauqua Lake

Athenaeum Hotel, Chautauqua Institution

Dutch fur trade along the Hudson River, seventeenth-century engraving

NATIVE AMERICANS IN NEW YORK

Many people are surprised to learn that twenty-first-century New York is home to several federally recognized Indian tribes and two state-recognized tribes. The two state tribes—the Shinnecock in Southampton and Unkechaug or Poospatuck in Mastic—both have small reservations on Long Island, but because they lack standing as a federally recognized tribe, they don't have the same rights of self-government as their Upstate cousins do.

The federally recognized tribes Upstate are all descendants of the Iroquois or Six Nations Confederacy. Four of the five founding members of the confederacy (the Tuscarora, who migrated from the Carolinas, joined the confederacy in the early 1700s) still have communities in their ancestral homelands. The Cayuga is the only founding tribe that doesn't have a federally recognized reservation in New York today.

Though the Indians at first were happy to trade with the European explorers and settlers who came into their respective territories, the "discovery" and subsequent settlement of New York proved devastating to their way of life. Disputes arose over land rights, and some still haven't been settled yet. In the French and Indian War, the Iroquois fought valiantly for their British friends, but the confederacy was split when the Americans began agitating for independence. Unable to remain neutral, the confederacy's Council Fire was covered and each member nation was allowed to choose its own path in the Revolution. Most chose to remain allied with the British; only the Oneidas and some Tuscaroras fought on the colonists' side. After the Revolution, though, the Oneidas and Tuscaroras fared no better than their Iroquois brothers.

For the past several decades, New York's government and residents have been struggling with land claims brought by these tribes, who argue that they were unfairly pushed off their homelands without due process or suitable compensation. In the meantime, the tribes have worked to restore their own economies, in many cases building casinos and using the revenues to provide housing, health care, educational opportunities, and other services to their members.

Many of New York's tribes share their culture and heritage through annual powwows and festivals, which usually feature dance competitions and exhibitions and traditional crafts and foods. From May to October, one can choose from about a dozen such festivals from Long Island to Glens Falls.

Iroquois Indians, 1914

Smoke dance competition, Native American festival, Saratoga Springs

Postcard view of trout fishing in the Finger Lakes region

Trout fishing on the Neversink River, Catskill Mountains

Hunting and Fishing

New York has always offered some of the best and most varied fishing on the continent. The Lenape fished the saltwater species in the Hudson River; the Iroquois went after freshwater fish in Oneida Lake and the myriad rivers and streams of Upstate. Fish that wasn't eaten immediately was salted and dried for use in the winter.

Through the 400 years since the first European settlers arrived, fishing for sustenance and for sport has been a constant. And small wonder: New York has hundreds of miles of coastline, various estuaries, 50,000 miles of rivers, creeks, and streams, and more than 7,500 lakes and ponds. These waters support a wide range of saltwater, cold-water, and warm-water fish. Lake Erie is known for its small-mouth bass, Lake Ontario is a haven for Pacific salmon, and Oneida Lake is famous for its walleye. Fly-fishing on the Salmon River is an annual ritual for thousands of fishermen. Spring on Long Island brings out anglers hoping to net Atlantic cod, mackerel, or winter flounder; in the summer, attention turns to bluefish, summer flounder, and Spanish mackerel. Striped bass, after suffering a period of low populations, also have returned in force to New York's coastal waters.

There are more than forty-five species of game and pan fish in New York's fresh waters, their numbers helped by the state's fisheries and stocking programs, which add one million pounds of fish to New York's lakes and rivers every year. And fishing isn't limited to warm weather: Lakes in the Adirondacks and elsewhere in the state are dotted with ice-fishing huts as soon as the surface can support a snowmobile or ATV to tow them out.

More than one million New York residents have state fishing licenses, and sport fishing contributes nearly $1.5 billion to the state's economy every year.

Outsiders don't often think of New York as an ideal locale for hunting and trapping, at least not in the twenty-first century. It's true that, for a time, overly aggressive hunting practices decimated many wildlife populations, virtually driving out beaver, wild turkeys, and other species. But conservation and wildlife management programs have restored both the animals and the habitats in which they live, and today New York has a broad range of big and small game hunting opportunities.

Before the Dutch began settling Manhattan, the Lenape and other Indians would hunt bobcat, bear, and deer on the island, and you can still hunt trophy deer in the New York City suburbs

Fishing in New York Harbor, Bay Ridge, Brooklyn

(although only bow hunting is permitted there). Small game, including rabbit, red and gray fox, squirrel, bobcat, turkey, and waterfowl, abound throughout the state, and trappers can target fourteen species of fur-bearing animals, from beaver and raccoon to mink and muskrat.

According to the state Department of Economic Conservation, about 750,000 people (including 50,000 from other states) hunt in New York every year. Trapping is less common, although it was a popular activity for youngsters until the 1960s. Today, the DEC reports that the number of licensed trappers ranges between 5,000 and 10,000 a year, depending on wildlife populations and the status of fur markets. Even so, the Empire State remains one of the nation's top producers of wild furs, most of which end up in the commercial fur trade.

Lake fishing, Adirondack Park, 1890

Birdseye view of Buffalo, 1880

BUFFALO

The Erie Canal established Buffalo as an important shipping and industrial center, and 125 years later, construction of the St. Lawrence Seaway took the city out of the shipping loop. In between, Buffalo was home to large steel manufacturers, grain production facilities, auto plants, and Great Lakes shipping concerns. It was once the fifteenth largest city in the United States, with a half million people, but it has lost residents every year since the 1950s as most of its industrial base left town. There are still remnants of the steel and auto industries, though they employ far fewer people than they did in the first half of the twentieth century, and for the past several years the city has concentrated its economic development efforts on a more diversified mix of light manufacturing, high tech, and service industries. The city also is building its reputation as a center for human genome research and other medical advancements through the Buffalo Niagara Medical Group, which includes University of Buffalo research teams and the Roswell Park Cancer Institute. The Seneca Indians, who recently opened a casino in Niagara Falls, have a small temporary slots hall in Buffalo and plan to open a permanent, full-service casino resort in Buffalo's Inner Harbor by 2010.

Buffalo is located in ancestral Seneca country. The Senecas were founding members of the Iroquois Confederacy and were known as the "keepers of the Western door," an analogy to the longhouse the Iroquois tribes typically lived in. The Confederacy saw itself as one big longhouse with the Mohawks at the eastern door and the Senecas at the western. The Seneca fought for the British during the American Revolution, and many of their villages were burned during Sullivan's Campaign after the war to punish the loyalist Iroquois and drive them out of New York.

Buffalo itself was burned by the British during the War of 1812, but the Erie Canal brought new shipping opportunities to what was then a village of about 2,500. Shortly after the canal was completed, Buffalo's population swelled to 10,000, and it received its city charter in the 1830s. Thanks to its nearly unlimited hydroelectric power source, Buffalo was the first city to introduce electric streetlights, thus earning the moniker "City of Light."

Buffalo harbor, 1925

Main Street, Buffalo, 1900

Main Street, Buffalo

Buffalo harbor

American Falls at Niagara Falls

NIAGARA FALLS

Humans have always been fascinated with Niagara Falls. It's the second-largest waterfall in the world (only Africa's Victoria Falls are larger), sending an average of 150,000 gallons of water every second over a 176-foot brink, roughly the equivalent of a twenty-story building. Because of its connection to the Great Lakes, it has always been of strategic importance—to the Indians, French, and British for the fur trade, and to the Americans for its entree to the vast expanse of the Ohio Valley and beyond.

To the first settlers of the area, the Falls were not merely an awe-inspiring feature of nature; they represented cheap, continuous power. Hydro power was quickly harnessed for manufacturing, and Italian and Polish immigrants flocked here in the 1800s to work at the multiple plants located along the Niagara River. Tourists came to gawk at the Falls, too, and in the winter they would even walk out on the natural ice bridge beneath the Falls—a practice that ended after 1912, when the ice bridge buckled and three tourists were killed.

American Falls at Niagara Falls, 1870 lithograph

Like many manufacturing towns, Niagara Falls saw most of its industry flee to places with cheaper labor and lower taxes after World War II. When the Love Canal neighborhood, which had been a landfill for chemical and industrial waste before it became a residential center, had to be evacuated in 1978, Niagara Falls' reputation as a run-down, unsafe place seemed sealed.

Opposite, bottom: *Tourists prepare to board* Maid of the Mist, *1908*

In recent years, however, state and local leaders have taken steps to re-establish Niagara Falls as a tourist destination, with growing success. Between eight million and ten million people visit the region every year, ranking Niagara Falls in the top ten U.S. destinations. The city boasts a new conference center and several redeveloped properties, as well as an extensive park system to give tourists the best views possible of the Falls, the river, and the spectacular gorge beneath the Falls. The Seneca Indians recently opened the Seneca Niagara Casino downtown, and a new Theater in the Mist and the Niagara Aerospace Museum are additional attractions.

Rainbow over Horseshoe Falls and Maid of the Mist

Newlyweds at Niagara Falls, 1894

View of American Falls from Cave of the Winds walkway

View of Niagara Falls from Hennepin Point, 1914

INDEX

ABOUT THE AUTHOR

Meg Schneider is an award-winning writer with more than two decades of experience in television, radio, and print journalism and public relations. The daughter of a history teacher, she has always been fascinated with connecting the past and present. Schneider has lived in Upstate New York since 1996, where she has written extensively about the state's history for newspapers, speaking engagements, and educational programs.

Her journalism honors include awards from the Iowa Associated Press Managing Editors, Women in Communications, the Maryland-Delaware-D.C. Press Association, Gannett, the New York State Associated Press, and the William Randolph Hearst Foundation.